Dawson City

Volume 15, Number 2 / 1988
ALASKA GEOGRAPHIC®

The Alaska Geographic Society

To teach many more to better know and use our natural resources

Editor: Penny Rennick
Associate Editor: Kathy Doogan
Editorial Assistance: Laurie Thompson
Designer: Sandra Harner

ABOUT THIS ISSUE: The development and growth of Dawson City is intricately intertwined with the story of the Klondike gold rush. To recount this colorful story, we called on Anchorage writer Mike Doogan, a lifelong Alaskan. His association with the gold rush began with his great-grandfather, John Egbert Feero, who lived in Skagway and operated a pack train carrying stampeders' goods over the White Pass Trail. Mike's interest in the area was rekindled in 1981 when he made a raft trip on the Yukon River, retracing part of the gold seekers' route, and ending in Dawson.

In addition to this account of Dawson's past and present, Ron Wendt details the lives of two Dawson sourdoughs and John Calam shares memories of his summer of 1947, spent working at Yukon Consolidated Gold Corporation's Granville Camp.

We thank the many fine photographers who contributed their images for this issue, and we are grateful to Lynn McPherson of Yukon Archives for her help with historical photographs. We also thank Linda Bierliemeir and David Neufeld of Parks Canada for their reviews of the manuscript.

COVER—*Dawson City, population 1,553, is situated along the east bank of the Yukon River at its confluence with the Klondike River. (H.J. Noyes)*

PREVIOUS PAGE—*Yukon Consolidated Gold Company's dredge No. 4 now rests on claim No. 17 Below Discovery on Bonanza Creek. The largest wooden hull, bucket line dredge in North America, Parks Canada has restored No. 4 and opened it to tourists. (Mike Doogan)*

ALASKA GEOGRAPHIC®, ISSN 0361-1353, is published quarterly by The Alaska Geographic Society, Anchorage, Alaska 99509-3370. Second-class postage paid in Edmonds, Washington 98020-9989. Printed in U.S.A. Copyright © 1987 by The Alaska Geographic Society. All rights reserved. Registered trademark; Alaska Geographic, ISSN 0361-1353; Key title Alaska Geographic.

THE ALASKA GEOGRAPHIC SOCIETY is a nonprofit organization exploring new frontiers of knowledge across the lands of the Polar Rim, learning how other men and other countries live in their Norths, putting the geography book back in the classroom, exploring new methods of teaching and learning — sharing in the excitement of discovery in man's wonderful new world north of 51°16′.

MEMBERS OF THE SOCIETY receive *ALASKA GEOGRAPHIC®*, a quality magazine that devotes each quarterly issue to monograhic in-depth coverage of a northern geographic region or resource-oriented subject.

MEMBERSHIP DUES in The Alaska Geographic Society are $30 per year; $34 to non-U.S. addresses. (Eighty percent of each year's dues is for a one-year subscription to *ALASKA GEOGRAPHIC®*.) Order from The Alaska Geographic Society, Box 93370, Anchorage, AK 99509-3370; phone (907) 258-2515.

MATERIALS SOUGHT: The editors of *ALASKA GEOGRAPHIC®* seek a wide variety of informative material on the lands north of 51°16′ on geographic subjects — anything to do with resources and their uses (with heavy emphasis on quality color photography) — from all the lands of the Polar River and the economically related north Polar Rim. We cannot be responsible for submissions not accompanied by sufficient postage for return by certified mail. Payments are made for all material upon publication.

CHANGE OF ADDRESS: The post office does not automatically forward *ALASKA GEOGRAPHIC®* when you move. To ensure continuous service, notify us six weeks before moving. Send us your new address and zip code (and moving date), your old address and zip code, and if possible send a mailing label from a copy of *ALASKA GEOGRAPHIC®*. Send this information to *ALASKA GEOGRAPHIC®* Mailing Offices, 130 Second Avenue South, Edmonds, WA 98020-9989.

MAILING LISTS: We have begun making our members' names and addresses available to carefully screened publications and companies whose products and activities may be of interest to you. If you would prefer not to receive such mailings, please so advise us, and include your mailing label (or your name and address if label is not available).

The Library of Congress has cataloged this serial publication as follows:

Alaska Geographic. v.1-
[Anchorage, Alaska Geographic Society] 1972-
v. ill. (part col.). 23 x 31 cm.
Quarterly
Official publication of The Alaska Geographic Society.
Key title: Alaska geographic, ISSN 0361-1353.

1. Alaska — Description and travel — 1959-
—Periodicals.   I. Alaska Geographic Society.

F901.A266   917.98′04′505   72-92087

Library of Congress   75[7912]   MARC-S

Table of Contents

Dawson City Update 1988

Not another book on the Klondike! Not another This Was Dawson! Those were our first reactions to the volume that follows, but in retrospect we realized there were two valid reasons we should produce this particular issue for our members.

First of all, from a standpoint of just good old-fashioned newspapering, plain reporting, it really was time for an update on things Dawson. Time has a habit of moving in ways we hardly notice and effecting great changes that we find difficult to see when we as editors have been in and out of the passing scene on things Yukon for a good many years, not really seeing change because we and ours were so often part of the change, and unconsciously still living in the memory world of things long gone by.

Dawson was and still is a wonderful place, but the old Dawson is something else today. That much is worth reporting and one rationale for this book.

On another front, we have undertaken a program of doing *ALASKA GEOGRAPHIC®*'s "from the headwaters of the Yukon to its mouth." We've recently done the Upper Yukon from the great river's first little beaver ponds beginnings. We've done the Koyukuk and eventually we'll move on downriver and complete for you a full Yukon River Library.

And no Yukon River Library would be complete without a good contemporary overview of Dawson . . . so . . . herewith, an updated recap for The Alaska Geographic Society of one of the most famous cities in the world.

Sincerely,

Robert A. Henning
President
The Alaska Geographic Society

INFORMATION
> CENTRE >
VISITOR RECEPTION CENTRE
FRONT ST
KING

Introduction

No ghosts live in Dawson City. Perhaps that's because so many of the men and women who lived there died elsewhere. The man who found the gold that sparked the Klondike rush, a Tagish Indian named Skookum Jim Mason, died at Carcross, Yukon, in 1916. The one who founded the town, a miner with a merchant's heart called Joe Ladue, was killed in 1898 by tuberculosis in Plattsburgh, New York. Of the two most famous "Kings of the Klondike," the first — another miner with a taste for real estate named "Big Alex" McDonald — was felled by a heart attack while looking for another fortune on Clear Creek, Yukon, in 1909. The second, entrepreneur and adven-

turer Joe Boyle, earned another title — "Savior of Romania" — before dying in Europe in 1923. One of the men who wrote best about the Klondike, Jack London, killed himself in Glen Ellen, California, in 1916; the other, Robert Service, died in 1958 in Brittany. Lively men, it is said, make restless ghosts. But no ghosts live in Dawson City.

Real people do, more than 1,500 of them at last count. They wear the city, built for more than 15,000, like a loose skin. On every street, around every corner are reminders of Dawson's past glory. Once the city was the stuff that dreams are made of, the place that 1 million people yearned to reach.

For two years just before the turn of the century, the gold rush blazed like a nova around the world. From Seattle and San Francisco, Chicago, New York, London, Brisbane and County Donegal, people were going to the Klondike! To Dawson! But like a nova, the rush burned out quickly. Most of the

One of the graves in a cemetery near Dawson is that of "Big Alex" McDonald. Although he is thought to have made $20 million during the period from 1896 to 1899, McDonald died a pauper in 1909. (Ron Wendt)

The Dawson Visitor Reception Centre, located on Front Street at King, is a replica of the Northern Commercial Company store which stood on the site from 1897 until it burned in 1951. (Rollo Pool, staff)

million never made it. Most of those who did were disappointed. There was not enough gold to go around.

Like the light from a nova, the gold rush still illuminates Dawson. Where miners and hurdy-gurdy girls once walked, tourists troop. The summer night, once alive with the howl of half-tame dogs, is filled with the growl of motor homes. The light from the past shines upon the tourist dollar, and Dawson lives on.

That in itself is an accomplishment. Bennett City is dead. So are Fortymile and Fort Reliance, Grand Forks and Granville, Hootalinqua, Fort Selkirk and Big Salmon, Klondike City and Nation City. The gold rush made and broke towns in the blink of an eye. Some are now just names, some just the scattered and collapsing cabins of the northern ghost town.

But Dawson City survives. This is its story.

ABOVE—*The old Palace Grand Theater, Arizona Charlie's showplace, is now home to the Gaslight Follies, an old-time variety show staged from late May to early September by the Klondike Visitors Association.*
(Rollo Pool, staff)

RIGHT—*The old Territorial Administration Building was built in 1901 and served as the seat of the government for Yukon Territory until the capital was moved from Dawson to Whitehorse in 1953. The building underwent a complete renovation in 1986 and now houses the Dawson City Museum.*
(Mike Doogan)

LEFT—*This large-scale mining operation, located off Bonanza Road, provides an excellent view of the famous White Channel Gravels, an ancient riverbed composed of pulverized talc and white quartz that contained great quantities of gold.*
(Mike Doogan)

BELOW—*Dawson City can be seen stretching quietly along the Yukon River in this photo taken from Midnight Dome. (Steve McCutcheon)*

The Miners Arrive

The Yukon River runs north, then west, for nearly 2,000 miles. Part of the land it drains, a part along the modern Canada-Alaska border, is called the Yukon Crystalline Terrane. This is a piece of land peeled off during the collision of two of the earth's great plates and welded to the North American continent by the force of the collision.

This particular piece of land contains gold. In the 100 million or so years after the land joined North America, the Yukon River and its tributaries cut the gold out of its host rock and washed it along. The beds of the rivers and streams became loaded with gold. When

A Native family gathers for a photo at their camp, three miles from Dawson, around 1898. The stampede drew Natives closer to the settlements, bringing about an end to their traditional lifestyle. (Photo by Arthur Albert Martin, Anchorage Museum)

they changed course, the old beds were covered over and the pressure of the land on top of them fused them into a kind of rock called conglomerate. The rivers and streams cut deeper, leaving these old beds as benches on hillsides.

Because the upper Yukon region was never covered by glaciers, the gold was not ground up and dispersed. When men finally found the gold, they found a lot of it. They called the gold-rich conglomerate the White Channel Gravel. It is being mined to this day.

The men hunting gold came north along the Cordillera, the collection of mountains, foothills, plateaus and valleys that stretches from the Rocky Mountain ranges to the Pacific. The 1849 strike in California brought the men west. Then they followed the spiny contour north, finding gold along the way.

Three of these prospectors were Arthur Harper, Al Mayo and Leroy Napoleon "Jack" McQuesten. In 1871 Mayo and McQuesten

left the Peace River country of British Columbia and headed north. "We had heard a great deal about the Yukon River from men that were in the H.B. [Hudson's Bay] Company employ," McQuesten wrote, "and concluded we would go and see for ourselves what the country was like."

Along the way they met some other prospectors, including Harper. None of the three made much money mining. But for the next 25 years they worked as traders, encouraging and directing other miners, extending them credit and shaping the rules of their society. They were the godfathers of the gold rush.

At first, Harper, Mayo and McQuesten joined the area's other white men in the fur trade. Since whites had arrived along the Yukon in 1789, fur trading had been the basis of the economy. At first the interior Natives, called Athabascans, traded through their neighbors — the Eskimos to the north and west and the Tlingits to the south. Later, with the establishment of Fort Yukon and, briefly, Fort Selkirk, they began trading directly with whites.

The group whose territory included the gold was the Han. When whites first arrived, about 1,000 Han were making a living from the 22,500 acres they controlled. Like the rest of the northern Athabascan groups, the Han spent most of their time trying to stay alive. Their primary food source was fish, of which the migrating salmon was most important. They caught the fish in dip nets and gill nets, and by building traps at the mouths of the Yukon's tributaries. One of those tributaries was a particularly good salmon stream, so the Han named it after their practice of driving willow pegs into its bed to hold the traps. They called it Hammer Water; in their language, *Tron-duick*.

Because they were dependent on fish for their subsistence, the Han spent most of their time along the rivers. The spring and summer were spent there, catching fish and drying them. In the fall, the men would go to hunt big game, while the women gathered berries. This diet was supplemented by such birds and small game as could be caught or killed. Winter was spent mostly in repose, although the men would go inland to hunt caribou again and to bring back cached meat.

The Han wore skins, caribou being the most common. They made bags and buckets of tree root and bark, and spoons of horn. Their weapons were bone knives, bone-tipped spears, and bows with bone-tipped arrows. Some of the Han most likely had weapons of copper, and perhaps iron, obtained in trade. They made deadfalls and

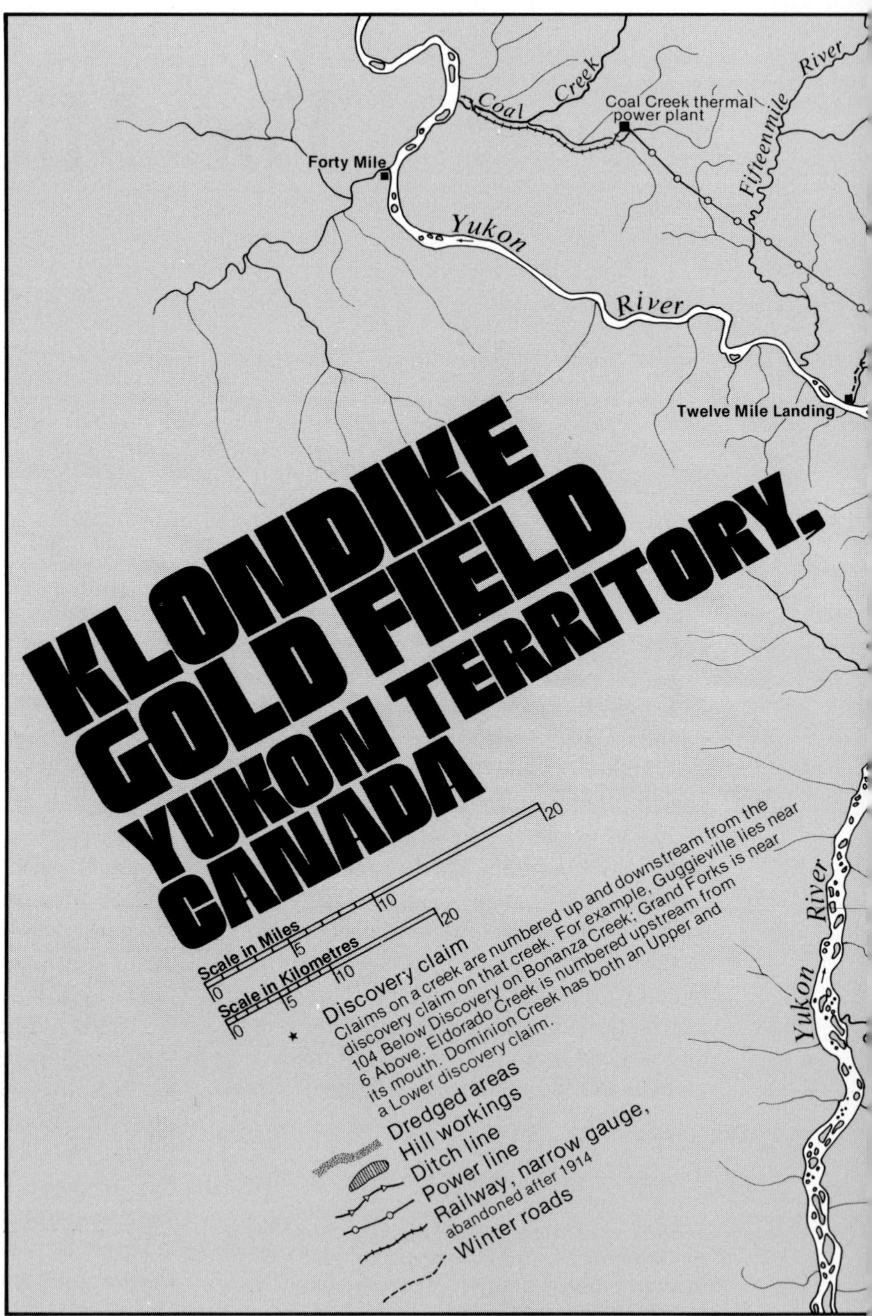

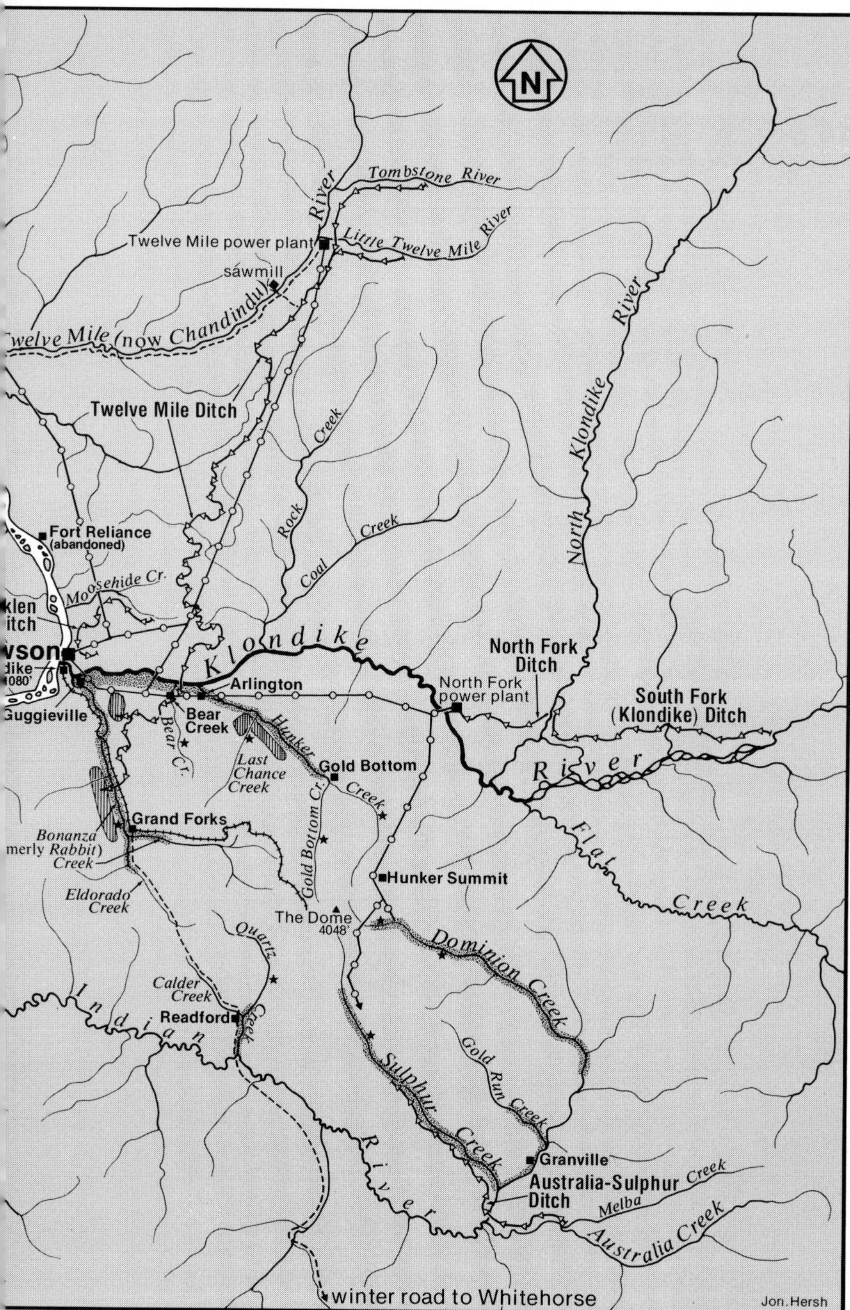

snares for traps. They decorated themselves and their possessions with feathers, quills and dyes. Depending on the season, they lived in moss houses or skin tents. They were accomplished rivermen and made fine birch-bark canoes. During the winter they traveled on snowshoes made of birch. If they used sleds before the whites arrived, they pulled them themselves.

To make fur trading easier, McQuesten's first post was set up across the Yukon from a large Han camp. Named Fort Reliance, the post was about six miles downriver from where the Tron-duick joined the Yukon. The miners measured distances along the river from Fort Reliance the same way they measured a creek from the discovery claim — in both directions. Thus the Fortymile River was 40 miles downriver from Fort Reliance, while the Sixtymile was 60 miles upriver.

With the coming of the miners, the area's economy shifted away from the fur trade. In

A group of local Natives sells a load of moose meat at Dawson in 1897 or 1898. The rush to the Klondike created many jobs for Natives; in addition to providing meat to the stampeders, they worked as guides, packers, laborers and woodcutters for the steamboats which plied the Yukon River. (Photo by Arthur Albert Martin, Anchorage Museum)

1880, the Tlingits, who controlled the White and Chilkoot passes through the Coast Mountains, let the first party of miners, 20 men from Juneau, through one of the jealously guarded passes. More followed. In 1885, paying quantities of fine, flour gold were discovered on the Stewart River. The next year other miners discovered richer diggings of coarse gold on the Fortymile River. This discovery led to the establishment of the first real white settlement on the upper Yukon. And if we want to understand Dawson City, we should pause for a moment and examine that settlement, Fortymile.

The Mining Life

Miners Keith and Wilson work their claim on French Hill, located just above Tom Lippy's rich No. 16 Eldorado. The man at the right rests on a windlass, a structure erected to hoist rocks to the surface. Once there, the gold was washed out in a sluice or rocker box like that being operated by the man on the left. (P.E. Larss Collection, Alaska State Library)

The men who mined the North were not a sociable lot. Many of them preferred the isolation of prospecting; in turn, the isolation sharpened whatever eccentricities had pushed them out of more settled society. So they made virtues of their defects by developing a society based on the most basic of individual freedoms, the right to be left alone. In the mining lifestyle, you could do what you wanted, as long as it didn't hurt another white man. Coupled with this was the most basic of individual responsibilities, to help others.

The life that developed around these twin precepts fits no neat category. It worked best among small numbers of men scattered over a large area. In such situations, a miner could seek out as much or as little company as he wanted, but could find help when he needed it. When the miners clumped together in larger groups, the life tended to deteriorate. When they clumped together with people used to other, more pragmatic, ways of living, it tended to evaporate.

The mining life was idealistic in theory, but rugged in fact. It often broke the health or spirit of a miner; sometimes it broke both. In the most practical, day-to-day sense, it was a way of living that separated the weak from the strong, then crushed the strong.

Fortymile was the essence of the northern mining camp. Its buildings were of green wood, usually logs, with moss to fill in the cracks, and sod roofs. They were low, ill-lit and poorly ventilated. Windows were covered with what was handy, often collections of jars stacked together; McQuesten tells of once using ice blocks and replacing them as they melted. Heat came from inefficient, wood-burning, sheet metal Yukon stoves, kept red-hot throughout the winter. The miner's wet clothes were often hung near the stove to dry, adding another aroma to the smell of wood, heat, unwashed men and poorly preserved food. The floors were generally of dirt. The usual furnishings were crudely made beds, a couple of chairs and a table. Bad light came from lamps or bitches, wicks stuck in fat.

The miners' diet was awful. They ate, when they had it, bacon, biscuits and tea. Their cooking arrangements dictated frying, so fresh meat was often partly raw. They had, most

One of the hardships early-day Dawson residents faced was their isolation from news of the outside world. Here, a group eagerly awaits delivery of the mail at the post office. (Special Collections Division, University of Washington Libraries, photo by Frank Newell, negative #X2263; reprinted from The Alaskan Gold Fields [1983])

of the time, no fresh vegetables. They never had fresh fruit. Milk, when there was any, was canned or powdered, as were eggs. The post at Fortymile was served by steamer, which came upriver from St. Michael. The boat couldn't carry much or make many trips, so supplies from Outside were limited.

At work, the miners spent a good part of their time wet. Searching for gold often meant a day spent knee and elbow deep in the frigid northern rivers and streams. Once gold was struck, it was harvested using water; water swirled in the big, pie-platelike gold pans; water was run through the cradlelike rockers, which shook the gold to the bottom for collection. Wherever there was a lot of gold, the miners built sluice boxes, long troughs narrower at one end so that they could be strung together. By running water through the boxes, the miners created imitation creeks. They shoveled dirt and rock into the sluices. The dirt and rock were washed away. The gold and other heavy metals washed out, sank and stuck in the riffles built into the sluices as gold traps.

In winter, when the water was frozen, prospecting and sluicing were out of the question.

Regardless of the payoff, most Klondike miners put in long days of hard and dirty work. This group of haggard souls was photographed working on bench (hillside) claim No. 14 Eldorado. (P.E. Larss Collection, Alaska State Library)

But the miners could stockpile dirt and rocks for sluicing in the spring, if they could break up the frozen ground.

Pick and shovel were useless. The miners could use them to strip off the vegetation that insulated the ground, but the sun made slow work of melting it. At Fort Reliance some miners had tried building a fire to melt the earth, and that practice was renewed at Fortymile during the winter of 1887. A fire could be banked, covered with green boughs, and left to burn. The miners would then dig away the thawed ground, lay a new fire, and repeat the process.

Fortunately for the Fortymile miners, bedrock lay close to the surface. They were not forced to dig 20 or 30 feet down, then "drift" a tunnel along the bedrock looking for the gold-bearing ore, the paystreak. So the gold was relatively easy to get at, and miners were spared hours in smoke-choked underground tunnels.

About all Fortymile had in the way of social centers were saloons: 10 of them. These were not the ornate, well-lit, airy pleasure domes of the movies. At Fortymile, the best saloon was not much different from the worst cabin. There were no dance-hall girls, no faro tables, often no whiskey. When the liquor ran out, the saloons served hootchinoo, a concoction of anything that would ferment. The miners called it hooch, cursed it and drank it hot.

This kind of living, combined with its general lack of sanitation and specific lack of medical care, produced the three scourges of the northern miner: scurvy, respiratory disease and alcoholism. Scurvy could be cured with spruce-bark tea. But lung disease, particularly tuberculosis, was a relentless

Much of the social life in early-day Dawson revolved around saloons. One of the first such establishments in town was the Bonanza. According to Tappan Adney, Harper's Weekly correspondent in gold-rush Dawson, the Bonanza's receipts were said to have frequently reached 100 ounces of gold dust, worth about $1,500, a day. (Photo by Sether, reprinted from The Klondike Stampede of 1897-1898 *[1900])*

killer of miners. So was alcohol, which made them stupid and careless.

Alcohol was an entrenched part of the mining life. A successful miner was expected to go on a spree, passing from saloon to saloon buying drinks for everyone he encountered. Only after his spree ended did he pay his bills or renew his supplies. During the spree, he was expected to look away as the bartender took the cost of the drinks from his poke; no one associated with the mining life was supposed to be dishonest.

When someone was found to be, the Fortymile miners convened a miners' meeting. The miners' meeting was the rule- and decision-making council of the American mining frontier. Miners' meetings set staking rules and tried men for murder, and did everything in

Patients, orderlies, nurses and doctors pose in Ward A of Good Samaritan Hospital. The second hospital built in gold-rush Dawson, Good Samaritan was established in August 1898 and partly funded by the Canadian government. Due to primitive sanitary conditions, deaths in the town at one time numbered three to four per day, and cases of malaria, typhoid, dysentary and other diseases kept the two hospitals full. (P.E. Larss Collection, Alaska State Library)

between. Like the miners themselves, the meetings could be — and often were — arbitrary and contentious. But for a time, they were the only law in the North.

Canada had more settled mining laws and a more formal, though often just as arbitrary, legal system. But no one was sure where Canada began, so the mostly American miners brought their meetings with them. Because the Canadians more or less ignored their northern holdings, there were no government officials with the power to oppose the meetings.

Fortymile offers a last glimpse of the mining life before it dissolved into the exaggeration of Circle and Dawson. It also displays some of the forces that were to destroy that life.

There was a woman at Fortymile, the wife of a miner named Tremblay, the first white woman over the Chilkoot Pass. Madame Emelie Tremblay was soon joined by others. The mining fraternity was just that, and the mining life celebrated male virtues, some of them adolescent. Wives would change that.

So would religion. The miners routed the first Anglican missionary sent to Fortymile, but Bishop William Bompas was as tough as any of them and he stayed. He held his services in a saloon and he drove a dogsled hundreds of miles to tend his flock. Since ministers were as fond of drunkenness, bad language and general immorality as wives, the churches, too, would alter the mining life.

As would the businessmen. John J. Healy had been just about everything there was to be on the Western frontier. When it became civilized he, like a lot of the people at Fortymile, just moved on. He had been running a trading post on the coast at Dyea when gold

A formidable deterrent to crime in the Klondike was North West Mounted Police (NWMP) Inspector Charles Constantine. Born in England in 1849, Constantine served in the army before enlisting in the NWMP in the 1880s. He established a post at Fortymile in 1895, where he served in a combination of jobs, including mining recorder, coroner and magistrate. When gold was discovered in the Klondike, Constantine recorded the claims and, with a contingent of about 30 constables, maintained law and order in the territory. He died while on leave in Long Beach, California, in 1912. (Photo by Arthur Albert Martin, Anchorage Museum)

was discovered on the Fortymile. The discovery convinced him there was real money to be made in the North. He in turn convinced others, including members of Chicago's Cudahy meat-packing family. Using their money, Healy formed the North American Trading and Transportation Company (NAT&T) and opened a post, named Fort Cudahy, across the river from Fortymile.

The miners welcomed Healy's wares, but they did not like his habit of expecting to be promptly paid. So when he was hauled before the miners' meeting by one of his employees, they ruled against him. That was a mistake. Fortymile was in Canada, and Bompas had been pestering the government for some law enforcement. When a substantial merchant like Healy added his request, the government had to agree. In 1894, they sent Inspector Charles Constantine of the North West Mounted Police to Fortymile. He was joined the following year by a detachment. Soon after, the Mounties put an end to the miners' meetings and began enforcing Canadian law. Civilization had come to Fortymile.

By then, the next big strike had been made at Birch Creek. Circle City grew up to service the miners. It was on American soil and was run American style, by the miners' meeting, and miners' style, with easy credit and legendary sprees. Circle was Jack McQuesten's town; he ruled it spiritually and commercially if not physically. By 1896, Circle City, with its population of 700, boasted of being the biggest log town in the world.

Four Men Find Gold

Success has many fathers, so the story of how gold was discovered on a lightly regarded river is pretty complicated. The generally accepted tale has a merchant, in this case Joe Ladue, telling a member of the mining fraternity, Robert Henderson, of an area he should prospect in the drainage of two Yukon River tributaries: The Indian and Tron-duick (by then called Klondike) rivers. Henderson went there and started prospecting.

Here the story departs from the well-worn path of northern gold discovery. Henderson picked the wrong place to look. He found gold — it seems to have been impossible not to along the upper Yukon — but not much of it, about 8 cents worth to the pan. This wasn't bad pay at the time, but it was not a promising sign that a bonanza lay below. Despite this, he named the creek Gold Bottom and began mining in earnest.

On his way back to Gold Bottom with sup-plies, Henderson ran across George Carmack and his two Indian brothers-in-law, Skookum Jim Mason and Tagish Charley. Following the miners' code, Henderson told Carmack about the find. Carmack, Jim and Charley, who were at the Klondike fishing, went to Gold Bottom, decided not to stake, and started back to the Yukon. On the way, on August 17, 1896,

Credited with being one of the first two men to discover gold in the Klondike, Canadian prospector Robert Henderson came to Fortymile by way of the mines in Aspen, Colorado, in 1894. Henderson, whom William Ogilvie described as a "true prospector," never realized any wealth from his discovery. He staked claim No. 3 above Discovery on Hunker Creek, was forced to sell it for a fraction of its value because of poor health and returned to his wife and child in Aspen in 1898. (Photo by Tappan Adney, reprinted from The Klondike Stampede of 1897-1898 *[1900])*

This photo, probably taken in 1899, shows flooded campsites along the crowded shore at Dawson City. Flooding was a hazard each spring, when ice breaking up on the Yukon and Klondike rivers created jams, forcing the water to back up and overflow its banks.
(P.E. Larss Collection, Alaska State Library)

Waiting their turns to register mining claims, a crowd of miners forms around the government building in Dawson. (Public Archives of Canada/PA-13413, reprinted from The Gold Hustlers [1977])

along the banks of Rabbit Creek, one of the party, most likely Skookum Jim, found gold. A whole bunch of gold, coarse gold, the sign of a fortune in gold: the first pan contained $4 worth. The three men staked claims and, without telling Henderson of their find, went to Fortymile to record them.

How much of this is true, nobody knows. Henderson's story was backed by the rest of the mining fraternity, who would not admit that a non-miner, let alone a non-white, could have made the biggest strike in northern history. Carmack had the indisputable proof of the gold, the discovery claim and the second claim the law allowed to the man who staked first. Skookum Jim had his word and that of his brother, Tagish Charley. That both were Indians did not weigh in their favor. Eventually, the Canadian government would credit the two white men with the discovery.

When Carmack and his companions got to Fortymile, the miners refused to believe he had found gold; they suspected a hoax. But they knew gold from every producing stream by sight and Carmack's gold didn't look like it was from any previous discovery. So they asked Canadian government surveyor William Ogilvie, who was at work marking the Alaska-Canada border, what he thought. Ogilvie told them he thought Carmack must have gotten the gold somewhere. That was enough for the miners. Fortymile was soon empty; the rush was on.

Ogilvie was one of the few who stayed at

Fortymile. On September 6, 1896, he wrote to his superiors: "I am much pleased to be able to inform you that a most important discovery of gold has been made on a creek called Bonanza Creek, an affluent of the river known here as the Klondyke." This was the first word of the strike that reached the outside world, but like many a government report it was filed and forgotten.

The destination of the Fortymile miners lay just south of the Klondike River and immediately east of the Yukon. The area was hilly and laced with creeks, all of which soon had names. Rabbit became Bonanza and one of its small tributaries was named Eldorado. The place where they came together was some of the richest ground in the Klondike. Dominion and Hunker, named for the German miner who staked its discovery claim, rounded out the big four. The Klondike River itself yielded gold, as did many of the other creeks. But no matter how hopefully named — there was a Nugget, a Rich, a Pure Gold, a Ready Bullion — none of them paid quite as well.

As more miners arrived, drawn by the rapidly spreading word of the strike, they found Joe Ladue had done some staking of his own. Mining had not been profitable for him, so he had switched to merchandizing. Ladue was operating the post and sawmill on the Stewart River in partnership with Arthur Harper when he heard of the strike. He rushed to stake not a claim but a townsite. The site was a flat, swampy area on the east bank of the Yukon, across the Klondike from the creeks, just below one of the area's many domes. This dome, called Midnight, was marked by a slide caused by water erosion from within. Ladue liked naming things after people with influence, and surveyors were the highest-ranking government officials in the area. His Stewart River post had been called Ogilvie. He named his new townsite after George Mercer Dawson, the man who had led the first Canadian survey expedition. There he set up his sawmill once again and began to carve out a town and a fortune.

The place he picked was hardly ideal. At roughly the same latitude as Fairbanks, it was cold much of the time, frost-free for an average of only 90 days a year. Winter cold snaps of 50 to 60 degrees below zero were common. It was a dry cold, because the location got an average of about 12 inches of rain and snow each year. To keep warm, the miners stripped the hills and valleys of the spruce and poplar and birch. They were so thorough that by the next year building logs had to be floated about 170 miles downriver from Fort Selkirk.

Despite these handicaps, Dawson would be the biggest and brassiest of the northern mining camps, the prime example of the mining lifestyle and the things that killed it. What the small miners' brotherhood had created in the isolation of the North was about to be washed away by a tidal wave of gold seekers with ideas of their own. Like so many things, the mining life was to be ruined by success.

During the gold rush, businesses sprang up quickly to accommodate Dawson's swelling population. Here, piles of bricks stand between a brick and lime business and a building housing Smith and Hobbs' contracting and undertaking businesses.
(P.E. Larss Collection, Alaska State Library)

First Winter

The miners who abandoned Fortymile in 1896 for the new diggings were acting as much on instinct as logic. Rushes were a part of the mining life, like bacon and being wet. A rush did not have to be based on an actual discovery; any old rumor would do, and often did. What sparked rushes was the same thing that led men to climb hill after hill to prospect: hope.

Within two weeks of the discovery, Bonanza Creek was fully staked, one 500-foot-long claim after another from headwaters to mouth. Eldorado was staked; so were Hunker and Dominion and so on. But hope is a fragile commodity. After the heat of the rush wore off, many of the miners began to have second, more practical, thoughts. Some had good claims back at Fortymile, others hadn't enough money or supplies to make it through the winter. Still others didn't believe the Klondike was really a good prospect. So they unloaded their claims and headed off to that obscure corner of history reserved for the faint of heart.

These skeptics were not alone. Much of the mining brotherhood was simply not impressed by the Klondike strike. When news reached Circle City, for example, the miners there sat tight. What would silence the skeptics was the proving of a claim. Someone had to dig down and find the paystreak, a tough, dirty, back-breaking and often heart-breaking job. Many of the claimholders weren't interested.

But some were. Clarence Berry and his partner, Anton Stander, started burning their way toward bedrock on No. 6 Eldorado.

A worker for North American Trading and Transportation Company looks over sacks containing $1.5 million in gold dust, ready for shipment to Outside mints. (Photo by Robertson, reprinted from The Klondike Stampede of 1897-1898 *[1900])*

Others soon followed. What they found in October and November was spectacular pay. Eldorado would prove to be the richest placer creek in history.

Another of the workers was Thomas Lippy, a former secretary of the Seattle YMCA who had come north in the spring to make his fortune. That decision had already cost him and his wife, Salome, their young son. So the couple worked No. 16 Eldorado feverishly. Early in December they hit bedrock, and their first pan was rich; it contained more than $2.50 in gold. Like the other miners who had struck, Lippy hired workers to enlarge the shaft and drift the tunnel, breathe the smoke and windlass the diggings to the surface to await spring.

There was gold everywhere on No. 16 Eldorado; the claim would yield $1.75 million in time. From the diggings piling up on the claim, Lippy collected a special pan of the richest ore. This "big pan" contained more than $2,000 in gold.

When word of it reached Circle City, the town evaporated. As in a lot of cases, "rush" is a misleading term for what ensued; the miners had to cover more than 200 miles of frozen Yukon River to reach Dawson City. Some set out right away; others waited until spring. Finally, even McQuesten moved to Dawson. Circle City had become the world's biggest log ghost town.

As miners arrived from all over the North, Dawson City grew. It was hardly impressive that first winter. Joe Ladue built a house-store-saloon and his sawmill made boards for other buildings, but the city was mostly tents, put up any which way on the frozen muskeg.

Ogilvie was invited to Dawson to survey the townsite. Just as important, he was asked to survey the claims along Bonanza and Eldorado. The miners' methods of determining the 500 feet Canadian mining law allowed were not precise, particularly during a rush. So Ogilvie, on the condition his decisions would be final, agreed. Since his survey was much more accurate than the original staking, it created "fractions," small parcels of land between the regulation-sized claims. These could be staked. A member of Ogilivie's survey crew, Dick Lowe, claimed one not far from where Bonanza and Eldorado met. The Lowe fraction was worth hundreds of thousands of dollars. Its owner was rarely seen sober again.

Drunk was not a cheap condition to be in that winter. Whiskey, cut with water to make it last, was $1 a drink. Nothing was cheap: a large and increasing amount of gold chased a small and decreasing number of goods. No steamboats had stopped at Dawson during the summer because there had been no Dawson. What food and other goods there were had been packed in. New arrivals might bring something to sell; more often, they just brought appetites and empty pockets. Nobody starved, but the Klondike's newly rich had few opportunities to flaunt their wealth.

Spring breakup brought about 1,000 new gold seekers, men who had climbed the passes, built boats and followed the ice downriver. They were bound for the Circle City goldfields, but Dawson intercepted them.

As water began to run in the creeks, the Klondike miners built sluices and began washing the diggings they had stockpiled. Gold from the sluices went into bags and boxes and trunks and anything else that

Thomas and Salome Lippy came to Dawson from Seattle in 1896, acquiring and developing No. 16 Eldorado, perhaps the richest claim in the Klondike. The Lippys helped touch off the rush to the Yukon goldfields in July 1897, when they traveled to San Francisco with $65,000 in gold. No. 16 Eldorado ultimately yielded the Lippys $1.75 million, most of which they lost in several schemes, including one to develop the Katalla oil fields near Cordova. (Arnold and Helen Nelson; reprinted from The Alaska Journal®)

would carry it. The rocks and dirt washed out the ends of the sluices to create the first piles of tailings that, in time, would make the Klondike goldfields look like the moon. When the first steamboats arrived in June, the miners took their gold to St. Michael, where they boarded a pair of ships, the *Excelsior* and the *Portland,* for Outside.

The Rush Begins

The *Excelsior* reached San Francisco July 15, 1897. As Tom and Salome Lippy took their $65,000 in gold to a private mint, word of the strike swept across the country. The *Portland* docked at Seattle two days later, creating a fresh wave of yellow prose to set men's pulses dancing, the most famous being the "ton of gold" described by a Seattle newspaper.

Word of the Klondike strike came to the ears of a nation ready to listen. The U.S. in the 1890s was in turmoil. Its population grew nearly 20 percent between 1890 and 1900, fed by immigration and new births. People came flocking in two directions: westward and to the cities. Oklahoma, opened to white

A dog team hauls drinking water along the Dawson waterfront in 1898 or 1899. Tents and boats line the shore in this early photo of the town.
(P.E. Larss Collection, Alaska State Library)

settlement in 1889, had a population of 400,000 by 1900. Between 1870 and 1900, Los Angeles grew from fewer than 6,000 people to more than 100,000; Detroit from about 80,000 to nearly 300,000.

A vast shift was occurring, the U.S. was changing from a rural, agricultural country to an urban, industrial one. Mechanization sharply reduced the number of people required to run a farm. Those who lost their jobs went to the city, where they competed with city dwellers and immigrants for jobs in the burgeoning factories. What they found there was not always pleasant; this was the America of the sweat shop and laissez-faire. While the U.S.'s industrial output soared, money was tight. All U.S. currency was redeemable in gold, which meant the amount of money in circulation was limited to the amount of gold the government owned. This kept farm prices low and made loans hard to pay back. It also, along with the competition

for jobs and the owners' lust for profit, kept wages low. These were the Gay Nineties only for those Thorsten Veblen described in 1899 in *The Theory of the Leisure Class.*

Most people were willing to listen when they were told that they, too, could be rich. Plenty were willing to tell them. The yellow journals of William Randolph Hearst and Joseph Pulitzer, locked in a terrific circulation war, outdid one another in superlatives. Their dailies and the other newspapers of the U.S. had a total circulation of 57 million. They were supplemented by cheap weekly magazines, like *McClure's, Munsey's* and *Harper's.* In short order, books about the Klondike, some "authored" by people like Joe Ladue and William Ogilvie, began to appear. That these books were often a pastiche of the irrelevant and the inaccurate did not hinder their sale.

So news of the Klondike strike was carried by eager tellers to receptive listeners. Euro-

A group of stampeders gathers in front of Cooper & Levy, Pioneer Outfitters, in Seattle. West Coast merchants competed to provide goods to the thousands of hopeful miners bound for the Klondike. (Special Collections Division, University of Washington Library; negative #UW1749; reprinted from Klondike Letters [1984])

peans got word by the new trans-Atlantic cable. People, as many as 1 million by the best estimates, began to make plans to go to Dawson.

Few of these gold seekers seemed at all concerned about their lack of mining experience. Nor did the prospect of a difficult journey to a cold and distant spot deter them. Men had rushed to California with as little experience and found fortunes. Other men, the argonauts' fathers and uncles, had gone off and fought the Civil War with as little preparation. Whole families had traversed the continent in wagons to build themselves new, more prosperous lives. The gold seekers were part of a generation that thought it could do anything because other people, people all around them, had.

They were abetted in their intentions by merchants after some of the decade's trademark fast bucks. If you were bound for the Klondike, you could buy almost anything almost anyplace. The merchants of San Francisco and those of Seattle sought to entice the Klondike-bound to depart from their cities and leave some money behind. "SEATTLE, WASHINGTON, is acknowledged to be the SHORTEST, CHEAPEST and BEST route to the Alaska Gold Fields and the large majority will come and outfit here," began an ad for one Seattle merchant. Likewise, Canadian cities touted "all Canadian" routes to the Klondike in the hopes of getting the business themselves. Seattle won most of the traffic and began a profitable relationship with the North that continues to this day.

Whole outfits, containing everything from a Klondike stove to a magnifying glass, were for sale by merchants in a number of cities. An outfit could be very elaborate — some included a folding boat, chamois underwear and two different kinds of soap. Cost varied considerably with where the outfit was purchased and what was in it, but a rough average was $250. The same outfit at Dawson would cost twice or thrice as much.

The would-be miner could buy some fabulous products. Gillespie, Ansley and Dixon of Toronto offered The Strohmayr Patent Sleeping Bag: "It is made up with outside cover of water-proof, also wind-proof duck, lined with Dog, a fur perfectly adapted for the purpose, being short and strong." There were Shorey's Patent Blizzard Resister Suits and The Slater Mining Boot: "Wears like wire."

The ports soon began filling up with gold seekers. To move them north, shipping companies brought in anything that would float, packed the argonauts aboard like sardines, and sent them off up the Inside Passage. "The men were packed like pigs between decks with no daylight and very little ventilation," wrote one gold seeker of a ship he decided to let sail from Seattle without him. The description could have stood for many of the barely seaworthy hulls that carried men and material and horses and dogs north at astounding profit. Passage cost anywhere from $30 on up, with fares of $100 not uncommon. Freight went along for 10¢ a pound.

One Year's Outfit for One Miner

Articles	Price in Dawson	Articles	Price in Dawson
500 pounds flour	$60.00	20 pounds Arbuckle's coffee	10.00
80 pounds beans	10.00	5 pounds black tea	6.25
25 pounds peas	6.25	5 pounds chocolate	3.75
25 pounds rolled oats	6.25	2 bottles lime juice	4.00
15 pounds corn meal	3.75	6 bottles Worcestershire sauce	4.50
1 case condensed milk, 4 dozen 1-pound cans	24.00	30 pounds lard	9.00
1 case cabbage, 2 dozen 2-pound cans	12.00	1 box macaroni, 12 pounds	2.00
1 case roast beef, 1 dozen 2-pound cans	9.00	12 pounds mincemeat	12.00
1 case corned beef, 1 dozen 2-pound cans	9.00	2 pairs rubber boots	18.00
1 case sausage meat, 2 dozen 2-pound cans	18.00	1 tin assorted cakes, 36 pounds	10.00
1 case turkey, 2 dozen 2-pound cans	12.00	4 boxes candles, 120 to the box	24.00
1 case tomatoes, 2 dozen 2½-pound cans	10.00	1 case baking powder, 2 dozen ½-pound cans	12.00
1 case string beans, 2 dozen 2-pound cans	12.00	6 bars washing soap	1.00
75 pounds bacon	30.00	5 bars toilet soap	1.00
50 pounds ham	22.50	15 pounds salt	1.50
25 pounds dried apples	6.25	1 case coal oil, 10 gallons	12.00
25 pounds dried prunes	6.25	2 lamp chimneys	.50
25 pounds dried peaches	7.50	100 feet of rope, ¾ or ⅞ (45 pounds)	18.00
25 pounds dried apricots	8.75	1 five-foot bull saw	6.00
25 pounds raisins or grapes	6.25	2 bull-saw files	1.50
100 pounds granulated sugar	30.00	1 pair arctic overshoes	4.50
1 keg pickles, 5 gallons	5.00	2 pairs felt boots	5.00
1 keg sauerkraut, 5 gallons	5.00	4 pairs woolen socks	4.00
5 gallons maple syrup	15.00	2 pairs moccasins	5.00
25 pounds evaporated potatoes	12.50	2 pairs water boots	5.00
15 pounds cheese	7.50	6 pairs skin mittens	15.00
		Total	550.25

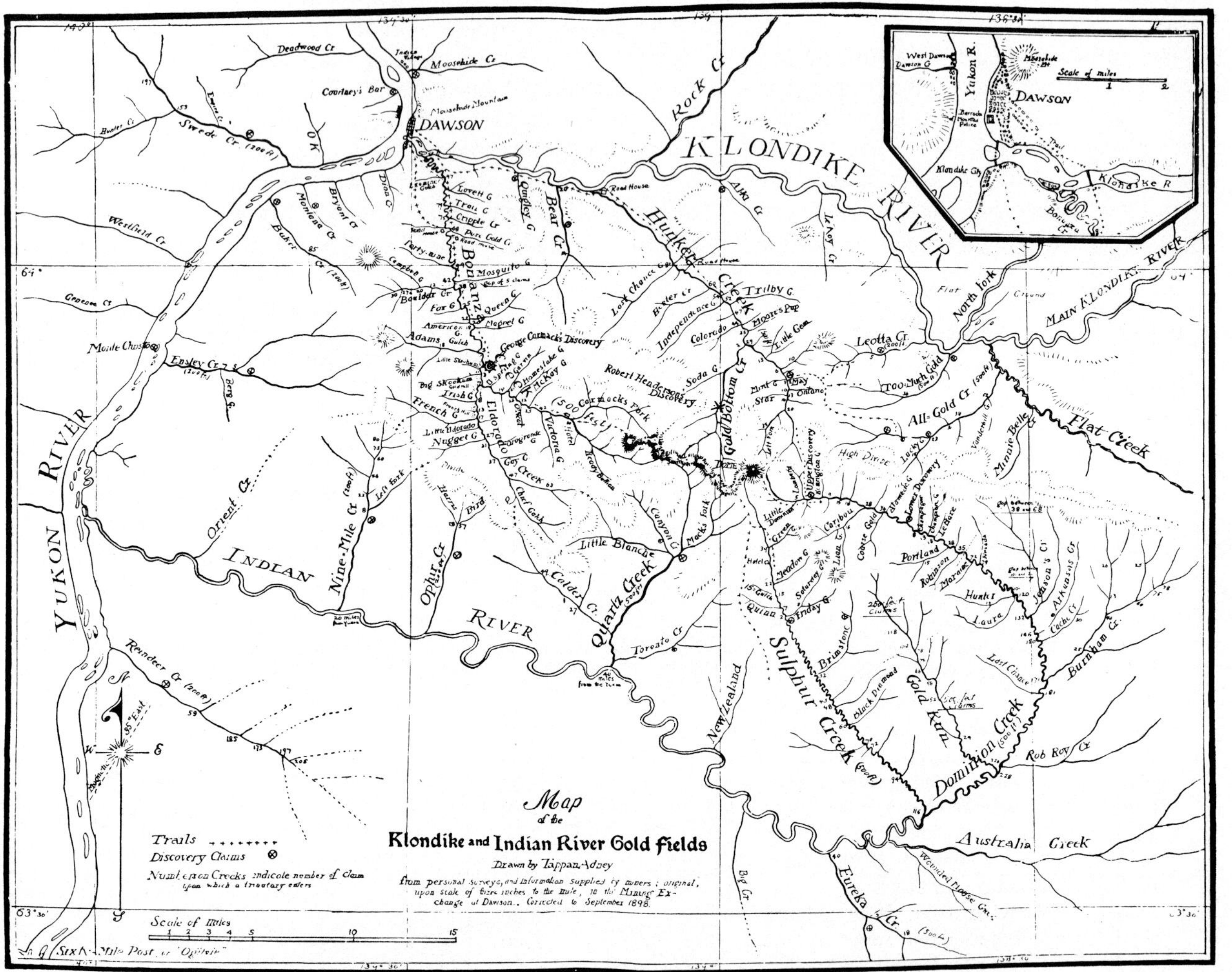

Harper's Weekly correspondent Tappan Adney drew this detailed map of the creeks between the Klondike and Indian rivers in 1898. (Reprinted from The Klondike Stampede of 1897-1898 *[1900])*

confusion. Once that was done, the men began the arduous task of transporting their outfits along the trails.

Those who chose the White Pass had to first run the gauntlet of Skagway. This was the domain of Jefferson Randolph "Soapy" Smith, con man and crime lord. Under Smith, Skagway was an obstacle course of confidence games and strong-arm robbery, watered whiskey and quick-fingered women. "There was plenty of everything in Skagway except morals," wrote a packer who worked the White Pass.

But not all the gold seekers chose the passes. The unwise and unlucky had plenty of other ways to try, and try they did. Some went all the way to St. Michael, then upriver to Dawson. Some tried the Stikine Route, some the Taku Route, following those rivers inland. Others tried to cross the glaciers at the head of Yakutat Bay and Valdez Arm. Some skipped the boats entirely, starting overland from Edmonton, Alberta, or Ashcroft, British Columbia.

Most of these routes were difficult; some were disasters. Those who left from Edmonton were two years on the trail. Those who tried the glaciers were turned back, often maimed or blinded.

There was even a toll road. Jack Dalton, as hard a man as the North has ever seen, built it, maintained it and enforced the toll, sometimes at the point of a gun. The Dalton

Most of these men ended up at either Skagway or Dyea, jumping-off points for the passes through the Coast Mountains that had once been the exclusive routes of the Tlingits. Once they reached these towns, the gold seekers were rushed off the boats by captains anxious to make the next lucrative trip. They found little organization and few facilities. So they formed their own landing parties and got their goods above high tide, where they lay in the mud in huge, jumbled piles while the men tried to extract their belongings from the

Trail ran from Pyramid Harbor (near present-day Haines) to rebuilt Fort Selkirk and was most often used to move cattle.

The passes were the quickest, most reliable route to the goldfields, but crossing them was no walk in the park. Except for a few of the more daring, the gold seekers were carrying their lives with them: food, tools, tents, sleeping bags, everything they needed to survive. There was no easy way to move this material. At first they tried horses. But the Chilkoot was too steep for horses. The White seemed more promising as a horse trail. It wasn't. Instead, the White Pass was a remarkably efficient horse killer; thousands died along its rocky, treacherous course, so many along one stretch it was named Dead Horse Trail. In fact, the White proved so bad that the gold seekers themselves closed it for repairs in August.

So most everything that went over the passes went over on men's backs, and the gold seekers began a bizarre relay race. Men would carry a load a distance up the trail, leave it, and return for another. Once their entire outfits had been moved to the new spot, they started over again.

They had a lot to move. When word of the gold strike finally penetrated the bureaucracy of the Canadian government, it reacted by sending more Mounties north. Although there was no agreed-upon border, the Mounties set up customs stations at the tops of both passes. Concerned about thousands of people arriving at the goldfields without enough to eat, they declared that each person going into Canada had to have a year's supply of food. The edict came in February 1898, long before many of the gold seekers could get over the passes.

The grueling White and Chilkoot passes to the Klondike were true tests of the gold seekers' dedication. The steep and muddy trails through the passes also took their toll on the pack animals. (Photo by Tappan Adney, reprinted from The Klondike Stampede of 1897-1898 *[1900])*

The food weighed more than 1,000 pounds. With clothes and tools, that made the average outfit about a ton. A man could carry a 65-pound load five miles in a day, then return to his outfit and do the same the next day. In a month, he could move his whole outfit that five miles. In five months, he could be at the Yukon River's headwater lakes.

Or he could pay others to do it for him. There were commercial pack trains. Some used mules, others men. And the Indians were packing as well, earning what was for them fabulous amounts of money at 5 cents to 50 cents a pound, depending on the season and the skill of the bargainers.

But no matter which route they took or how hard they tried, few of the 100,000 or so who actually set out for Dawson reached it in 1897. Winter arrives early in the North, and winter is no time to be traveling. Only those who moved quick and traveled light made it to Dawson.

RESTAURANT
MINERS HOME
THE PALACE

Second Winter

As the hordes moved north, the residents of Dawson spent summer 1897 digging gold. The miners dug it from the ground; everybody else dug it from the miners' pockets. On the creeks, the miners' cabins were cheek-by-jowl with their sluices and firewood piles; once outside their front doors, they were at work.

Dawson grew just as randomly. There was Dawson City proper, built on the Ladue townsite. Across the Klondike River was Klondike City, known as Lousetown; across the Yukon River was West Dawson. Along the main streets of Dawson — Front to Third, King to Princess — logs from the forest and boards from Ladue's sawmill were being turned into buildings. The lots they sat on had

Stampeders congregate along the boardwalks of Dawson in October 1897 as the second winter sets in. (Photo by Arthur Albert Martin, Anchorage Museum)

cost $5 the previous fall, but as more people arrived and more buildings rose, their value climbed. Saloons sprang up like mushrooms. Both the Alaska Commercial (A.C.) Company and the North American Trading and Transportation Company (NAT&T) opened stores. Bakeries and laundries and one-arm restaurants blossomed. The hordes may not have arrived, but it seemed everybody north of 53 degrees was crowding into the town.

Out on the creeks, near where Eldorado met Bonanza, another town was growing. This was Grand Forks, the creation of a woman named Belinda Mulrooney. She had been working on a ship that sailed the Inside Passage when she heard about the Klondike strike, so she was able to get to Dawson in the summer of 1897. She sold some goods that she had brought with her and, after deciding that there was too much competition in Dawson, moved out to the creeks and started building a hotel. Others followed.

Dawson was miles from the creeks, a three-hour commute on foot. Grand Forks, closer, prospered. So did Belinda Mulrooney.

So did many others. All the miners along lower Eldorado were rich, so were many on Bonanza, Dominion and Hunker. They were, most of them, not men of great intellectual attainments; perseverance and luck were as important as brains in determining who got rich. So many of the miners used their wealth the way much smaller amounts of money had been used at Fortymile and Circle City: they went on sprees.

But already the mining life was being changed. The bartenders used wet fingers to weigh out the gold on scales that were not true. "Champagne" sold for $60 a bottle and the hurdy-gurdy girls who had begun arriving worked hard to sell it. Professional gamblers ran poker games and faro layouts, not all of them strictly honest.

It wasn't just claim owners who had

Miners and others stand in front of the Magnet, one of many roadhouses which sprang up to provide meals and beds for the miners on the creeks east of Dawson City, in 1898. Some historians believe that Belinda Mulrooney, a Pennsylvannia coal miner's daughter who went on to become one of the legends of the gold rush, built the Magnet. (Yukon Archives, E.A. Hegg Collection; reprinted from The Alaska Journal®*)*

A group of miners poses with a hydraulic monitor on their claim No. 24 Below on Hunker Creek. (Courtesy of Nicki Nielsen)

money, either. There were the hired hands, working on other men's claims at $1.50 an hour, and laymen, the mining equivalent of sharecroppers, who worked other's claims for a share of the gold they found. There was no shortage of gold to move from one pocket to the next.

But there was a shortage of practically everything else. Water in the Yukon River was low that summer, and the steamboats from St. Michael got stuck. Since the first steamboat had chugged up the Yukon in 1869, the small, shallow-draft craft had been the mainstay of the supply network. But there were enough boats to supply hundreds, not thousands. Even if they managed to unstick themselves and reach Dawson, they'd be able to make only one trip. In Dawson, men began to worry about starving to death.

The A.C. Company told everyone who would listen to leave. Charles Constantine, the Mountie Inspector, decided Dawson would have to be partially evacuated. Most of those who left started downriver for Fort Yukon, but at least one party went upriver

and actually made it to Skagway, boarding a ship that had just finished disgorging another load of gold seekers.

Many of those who were forced to flee had just arrived; to get to the goldfields first, they had not carried the provisions necessary to stay. One was a U.S. Department of Labor employee named Sam Dunham, sent north to find out what was going on in the nation's northernmost territory. Dunham got to Dawson September 23, 1897, landing ". . . at the upper end of town, which is located in a swamp and oppressively crude." It was the middle of the starvation scare. On October 1, he left aboard the *Bella* for Circle City. He would make something of a name for himself as a poet of the gold rush.

Even with the departures, the food situation at Dawson was not good.

For one thing, people kept arriving. One was Tappan Adney, a keen observer who went north as a correspondent for *Harper's Weekly*. During his 92-day journey, Adney managed to stay one step ahead of the horde. He reached Dawson just before freeze-up, on October 31. "The town of Dawson, now just one year old, contains about 300 cabins and other buildings . . ." he wrote. There he found flour, which normally sold in the North for $6 to $10 a 50-pound sack, ". . . sold on the street for from $75 to $125 per sack of 50 pounds. . . ." because of its scarcity.

For another, many of those who left Dawson were forced to return; there were few

A customer pours gold dust from his poke to pay his bill at a Dawson lunch counter in 1899. As gold dust was the most common form of currency, scales were present on the counters of most establishments. (University of Washington Historical Photograph Collection; reprinted from The Alaskan Gold Fields [1983])

provisions anywhere along the river. Others stopped where winter caught them, Dunham wintering at Circle City. All along the river they clung to life, rationing their food and trying to stay warm. They were scattered in the same way the gold seekers were, at least those who had made it over the passes. Some stopped at Fort Selkirk. Others, including Jack London, wintered on the Stewart River.

Word of the food shortage reached the Outside. Driven either by a faulty sense of geography or a concern for the many Americans in Dawson, the U.S. Congress voted $200,000 for famine relief. Unfortunately, Congress, at the urging of missionary Sheldon Jackson, used most of the money to buy 539 reindeer in Lapland. What with transportation delays, the lack of reindeer moss and other perils, the reindeer proved a classic example of too little, too late: only 114 survived the trip. They arrived in Dawson in January 1899. What one author dubbed "the reindeer fiasco" did turn out well for one participant. A Norwegian who made the trip with the reindeer, Jafet Lindeberg, was one of the three men to discover gold at Nome.

Residents of Dawson knew nothing of Congressional plans. "Six thousand souls wintered in Dawson, of whom five-sixths did not know whether their stock of provisions would last till Spring," Adney wrote.

It wasn't just people who would go hungry. The miners had learned from the trappers who had learned from the Eskimos to use dogs to pull sleds. The Indians had learned it, too. So all along the Yukon there were dogs, dogs who were often hungry, dogs who would eat nearly anything. Caches were used as much to keep food, candles, fat and skin clothing from the dogs as to keep them from marauding bears. Often, the dogs were left to shift for themselves during the summer. Often, in the depths of a tough winter, it was the dogs who were eaten. Dawson was no different from any other northern settlement. "Dawson is, in the main, a city composed of grown people and dogs," Adney observed.

Scarcity of provisions did not put a stop to either mining or prospecting. The sourdoughs stuck mainly to mining, taking time out about once a month to stampede to some nearby and worthless locale. But the newcomers, barred from the creeks by their late arrival, kept prospecting. One of the things that drew their attention was the benches on the hillsides along the creeks. In the fall, a pair of tenderfeet, Nathan Kresge and Albert Lancaster, struck gold on the hillside above Lowe's fraction. Other miners immediately rushed to stake, but little mining was done. A second stampede followed in March, when another late arrival, William "Cariboo Billy" Dietering, discovered gold above No. 16 Eldorado. Finally, another cheechako, Oliver B. Millett, struck gold on the hill above Carmack's discovery claim. By breakup all the hillsides were staked.

The old-timers had thought the greenhorns foolish for looking on the hillsides because, they said, the weight of gold meant it could only be found on bedrock. But the newcomers looked at the benches and saw the beds of older watercourses. There they found the White Channel Gravels, which contained a fortune in gold.

If there was a lot of hard working and hard thinking going on, there was a lot of hard living and hard drinking, too. At the saloons of Dawson and Grand Forks the newly rich miners behaved in a way that Thorsten Veblen would have recognized: they consumed conspicuously.

As if their real exploits weren't enough, they grew in the retelling. Big Alex McDonald owned claims on all the gold-producing creeks, but the oral historians of the place made him even richer, dubbing him "King of the Klondike." If Swiftwater Bill Gates was extravagant in his courtship of a hurdy-gurdy girl named Gussie Lamore, the story became a tale of Gates cornering the market in eggs to win Gussie's affections. The dim and dirty saloons became pleasure palaces, the dance-hall girls turned into beauty queens.

Everything was bigger than life in Dawson City in the spring of 1898. "Persons regarded themselves as particularly cleanly if they changed underwear every two weeks," Adney wrote. But that reality was submerged in the growing mythology of Dawson, a mythology strong enough to withstand the wave of humanity about to wash over the town.

"Big Alex" McDonald came to the Yukon in 1895, first working for Alaska Commercial Company in Fortymile then moving to Dawson. McDonald was an imposing individual whose simple face and slow manner of speaking belied his shrewd business sense and thorough knowledge of mining. He took a fortune in gold from the Klondike, using the money to buy more claims and to hire others to work them for him. One of the men known as "King of the Klondike," McDonald was also generous, never refusing to lend money to a friend in need, and always willing to contribute to civic causes. (Photo by Arthur Albert Martin, Anchorage Museum)

The Rush Arrives

The trail over Chilkoot Pass ended at Lake Lindeman; the one over White Pass at Lake Bennett. As winter progressed, more and more men found themselves at the lakes, living in tents and building boats.

To get there, they had had to improve both trails dramatically. When snow fell, they cut stairs to carry their goods over the steep parts, returning for new loads by sliding back down

Following an 1897 fire in Dawson, two men sort through steaming ashes in search of nails. During the gold rush building materials were precious, nails ranging in price from about $6 per pound in 1897 to 25 cents apiece following the devastating fire of April 26, 1899. After a fire, opportunists "panned" the ashes, ostensibly in search of nails, but always on the lookout for gold or other valuables the blaze did not consume. (Photo by Arthur Albert Martin, Anchorage Museum)

on their bottoms. The stairs on Chilkoot Pass were called "The Golden Staircase," and one picture of men climbing them is the most famous ever taken in the North.

The way to the lakes was not just difficult; it could be expensive as well. The North West Mounted Police collected a customs duty equal to about 20 percent of the value of the gold seekers' outfits, an average of about $50. If they had their goods packed by professionals, they paid anywhere from $100 to $600.

The passes were dangerous for people as well as horses. An avalanche struck the Chilkoot in April 1898, killing more than 60 people. But when the pass was closed for three days while the bodies were hunted, the travelers chafed. If anyone was afraid of another avalanche, that fear did nothing to stop the procession once the pass was reopened. These people meant to get to the goldfields.

Once at the lakes, the task changed from packing to boat building. To cut lumber for the boats, the men had to erect saw pits, which were raised platforms on which to rest logs. Then they had to whipsaw the logs into boards, "the supreme test of the stampede," according to the Klondike's premier historian, Pierre Berton. One man stood on top of the log to guide the saw and lift it for the next cut, while another stood at the bottom to pull it through the log. Each thought he had the harder task and, since neither could see the other, there were many accusations of shirking.

All that winter men arrived at the lakes and built boats. Along the shoreline tents were mixed with saw pits and half-finished boats of every description. By the time spring arrived, 7,124 boats — the methodical Mounties had numbered each one — were ready to carry about 30,000 people to the goldfields. By the last day of May 1898 the lakes were

clear of ice and the largest fleet the North has ever seen was under weigh.

The people it carried — overwhelmingly but not entirely men — were the survivors of a rigorous weeding-out process. Of the estimated 1 million who had made plans to go to the Klondike, probably 100,000 actually started. Of these, 50,000 or so reached northern soil. Some looked at Skagway and quit right there, lining the beach with outfits for sale. Others were culled by the trials of the trails. The 30,000 who left Bennett were the majority of those who would reach the goldfields, the main body of the gold rush.

One of the boats was the *Iowa*, a 60-foot-long, 18-foot-wide sternwheel steamer. She was one of two boats built by a group of men from Alton, Iowa, that winter. The *Iowa* was carrying a tremendous amount of cargo: "... wood, weighing 25,000 pounds; also about 5,000 feet of extra lumber; ten horses weighing 11,000 pounds; hay for the horses; our heavy sawmill machinery, sleds and all provisions. Besides this we have six boats lashed to our sides...," wrote her captain, E.G. Abbott. The *Iowa* carried so much cargo that to have it moved around Miles Canyon on the tram at 1 cent a pound cost $1,000.

P.E. Larss, one of many photographers who documented the gold rush, was photographed bundled on his sled with camera equipment and his famous dog team in 1898. (P.E. Larss Collection, Alaska State Library)

A group of gold seekers from Alton, Iowa, works on the 60-foot-long, 18-foot-wide sternwheel steamer which would carry them from Lake Bennett to the Klondike goldfields. They arrived at Dawson in June 1898, finding "no work at any price and no money nor any way of earning it." *(Photo courtesy of Jack Wells; reprinted from* The Alaska Journal®*)*

One of the postcards gold seekers could send home was this view of a gold pan containing $6,000 worth of nuggets. *(Courtesy of Nicki Nielsen)*

Some of the party were worried that a boat so big could not get through the rapids, but that concern proved groundless. "Just a line to tell you that we have successfully run the White Horse Rapids and not a scratch to the paint on the *Iowa*," wrote Abbott. The *Iowa* reached Dawson June 23.

But the *Iowa* was not typical of the gold rush fleet, which contained boats of every size and degree of seaworthiness, each on average big enough to carry four people and their outfits. More common were boats like the *Michigan*, named for the home state of one of her builders, Alfred G. McMichael. Of her construction, McMichael wrote: "I never built a boat or saw one built and yet, we have one here which is all my own planning. It is a nice model and fairly well put together considering that lumber is rough and uneven and a week ago or a little more was standing in a

tree." McMichael and his partners lost the *Michigan* when it floated off, but found her again and, much relieved, set out for Dawson.

The *Michigan* was 23 feet 7 inches long and 5 feet 6 inches wide. She carried the three partners and all their gear across Lake Tagish, along Six Mile River, across Lake Marsh, and along Thirty Mile River to Miles Canyon. Here, Mountie Inspector Sam Steele had issued a decree: women could not shoot the rapids; they had to get out and walk.

The Mounties inspected each boat to see that it was capable of shooting the canyon. They also checked the men who proposed to pilot the boats. Steele had made up all the rules on the spot because in the first couple of days of the fleet's passage, 150 boats had been wrecked.

McMichael and his mates sent some of their load by tram at a cent a pound, hired a pilot

By the time this photo was taken, after July 1898, the Yukon Telegraph Company had provided telephone service to Dawson residents. The large log building was the office of Yukon Gold Company; buildings on either side belonged to Northern Commercial Company. (Courtesy of Nicki Nielsen)

for $15 and put the *Michigan* through. That was about all the excitement on the trip. McMichael's letters describe a boat trip both beautiful and, except for the mosquitoes, serene until, on the morning of June 20, 1898, the *Michigan* reached Dawson City.

The day before he arrived in Dawson, McMichael wrote: "The responsibilities of the whole trip now begin. All before has been only preparatory." But the reality of Dawson proved quite different.

Paris of the North

The vanguard of the stampede hit Dawson on June 8. They and those who followed them washed over the city like a wave. Dawson's 8,000 grew to 10,000, then 15,000, then 20,000, then more. The *Michigan* could not be moored to the shore because the shore was lined with boats, two and three and four deep. "The hillsides were white with tents and the streets black with a crowd of men," McMichael wrote. And Adney, who had weathered the winter well despite the food shortages, took himself off to look at the newcomers: "It is a motley throng — every degree of person gathered from every corner of the earth, from every State of the Union and from every city — weatherbeaten, sunburned, with snow glasses over their hats, just as they came from the passes."

They had reached the Klondike.

Unfortunately, the reality of the Klondike was not anything like the dream that had drawn them on. Dawson's streets were not paved with gold; they were not paved with anything. "The streets are vile," McMichael wrote. "Black mud or dust among logs and stumps." An American divorcee who arrived the next month found little to please the eye. "Everywhere were rough board buildings on stilts; hurriedly pitched tents, with stoves, cooking utensils, and bundles thrown around; and freshly cleared lots, with new one-room shacks, bushes, and shavings strewn about," wrote Martha Black.

The prospects were as displeasing as the view. The claims had all been staked, the gold was being dug for the profit of other, luckier, men. Prices were high: an egg cost $1, a gallon of milk $30, tobacco, $7.50 a pound. Laundries charged 50 cents for each piece of clothing. A pound of beef was $1; liquor, $50 a bottle; a copy of Shakespeare, likewise, $50. For those without income, Dawson was not the place to be. In McMichael's words: "Men, on arrival here, have suddenly found out that the unlimited opportunities for getting suddenly rich will not be realized no matter how great their capacity for enduring work and hardships."

In some bizarre way, the bulk of the stampeders were tourists, the Trail of '98 a sort of rigorous, expensive, dangerous group

Jimmy's Place, once considered to be the largest and best store in Dawson, offered a wide variety of local and exotic fruits and vegetables in addition to more mundane items such as postcards, magazines, stationery and soft drinks. (University of Washington Historical Photograph Collection; reprinted from The Alaskan Gold Fields [1983])

tour. The trip was all in the getting there. "This is wonderful country," the *Iowa*'s Abbott had written prophetically from Lake Tagish, "and if I do not get one ounce of gold, I will feel fully repaid for the trip." The gold seekers, like their fathers who had left home to fight the Civil War, went to see the elephant. Now that they had seen it, they weren't sure what to do.

Some turned around and headed straight back home. Others, like McMichael who spent only five days at Dawson, decided to try their hands at prospecting elsewhere. Still others went to work on other men's claims. Those who left were soon replaced by new arrivals. Maybe 30,000 people passed through Dawson that summer, maybe 40,000. Estimates of the city's population on any one day ranged from 15,000 to 25,000. A Mountie census put the population at 16,000, not including those who lived on the creeks. Even that figure made it by far the North's largest city.

As they passed through it, the gold seekers imbibed the place's mythology. At night, from the floors of the dance halls and saloons, they could look up at the gold kings in their boxes, treating the overaged girls to champagne of questionable vintage and caviar from unknown fish. They were heroes, these gold kings: Swiftwater Bill and Big Alex, Dick Lowe and Antone Stander and Clarence Berry. The girls were famous as well: Cad Wilson, Gussie Lamore and her sister, Nellie the Pig, Diamond Tooth Gertie and the Oregon Mare; working girls with working names who, if they weren't beautiful, at least were there.

They worked at saloons thrown up with

ABOVE—Frozen hog carcasses from Bennett are unloaded on the Dawson shore October 21, 1899. (Selid Collection, University of Alaska Archives)

RIGHT—Lucille Elliot, a dancer called the Swedish Queen, posed for this portrait in Dawson in 1897 or 1898. Dance-hall girls had much more freedom than the prostitutes who lived on Paradise Alley and later in Lousetown, across the Klondike River. (Photo by Arthur Albert Martin, Anchorage Museum)

Crowds of spectators line Front Street in Dawson for the town's first horse race, held May 24, 1900. Just one year earlier, in April 1899, a devastating fire had gutted the business district, destroying 117 buildings. (Selid Collection, University of Alaska Archives)

dispatch to catch the gold being flung around by the miners. Harry Ash had opened the first saloon-only building in Dawson, the Northern, the previous June. By the time the rush arrived it had been joined by, among others, the Monte Carlo, the M&N, the Combination, the Can Can and the Chisolm, where each drink was accompanied by a whisk for the drinker to use to brush himself off after he came to. Behind the saloons and dance halls were the cribs of Paradise Alley, where sturdy prostitutes, many of them Belgians, serviced the miners.

Dawson became, this big gold rush summer, a city to lighten the loads — and the pokes — of the Klondike's gentry. Out on the creeks, Clarence Berry had discovered that steam would melt the earth better than fire, so the gold was being dug more efficiently. In town, a good dance-hall caller could squeeze more than 100 short, $1 dances into an evening with time left over for drinks between. In town, gold was being dug more efficiently, too.

In the process a city was being built. Dawson City was founded on equal parts greed and free enterprise and they worked quickly. In addition to the saloons and dance halls, fine hotels were going up — Belinda Mulrooney's Fairview was the finest.

At its height, the town boasted five newspapers. One of the first had been a one-

A driver prepares to deliver a wagonload of kegs of beer from the Klondike Brewery in Klondike City in this photo, probably taken between 1906 and 1914. In the background are engines of the Klondike Mines Railway. (Public Archives of Canada/C-16904, courtesy of Nicki Nielsen)

ABOVE—*As residents and guests stand by, smoke pours from a fire at the McDonald Hotel on November 1, 1901. (Selid Collection, University of Alaska Archives)*

RIGHT—*Longest-lived of the many newspapers to come and go in Dawson, the* Dawson News *was published from July 31, 1899, through 1953. (Courtesy of Nicki Nielsen)*

shot publication produced by the flamboyant, self-promoting Arizona Charlie Meadows. His *Klondike News,* published April 1, 1898, was a vanity paper. For a fee, he printed the life stories of miners who had struck it rich. The single edition made Meadows about $50,000.

There were also bakeries, dress shops and laundries; anything that could make money was built. The $5 building lots were worth $8,000 a running foot along Front Street. This was Dawson at its height, the bubble before it burst. This was the Paris of the North.

For most of the year between the summers of 1898 and 1899, there was more poetry that truth in the label. Dawson's buildings were wooden and low; many of them showed false fronts to the world. Its streets were unpaved, its residents uncultured. There were no sewer or water lines. Dawson had no factories, it served no farms. It was, and would remain, a mining camp.

But, for that year, what a mining camp it was. The world had not before seen its like and would not see it again. In the summer of '98, the golden path led straight into town. As a result, Dawson flourished. It survived a fire in November 1898 that ravaged downtown. The gold kings continued to spend with both hands, many spending and investing their way back to poverty. They drove expensive teams of matched dogs, hired halls and steamers for parties and lost thousands of dollars on the turn of a card. Of the original group enriched by the Klondike find, few would die with any money.

All through the winter Dawson's spree continued. The Oatley Sisters, who were really mother and daughter, sang sentimental songs

The great number of saloons, dance halls and theaters which Dawson supported, and the fact that 120,000 gallons of liquor were brought in during 1898, demonstrate how important entertainment was to the boomtown. This 1898 view of Front Street shows the popular Monte Carlo next door to the Horseshoe Saloon, which housed the Oatley Sisters' Concert and Dance Hall. Polly and Lottie Oatley, actually mother and daughter, rose to success singing sentimental ballads and dancing with lonely miners. (Photo by Tappan Adney, reprinted from The Klondike Stampede of 1897-1898 *[1900])*

Gold was everywhere in Dawson, even around the waists of the town's ladies. Jeweler Albert Mayer made this gold nugget belt for Miss Rose Blumkin in September 1899. (Selid Collection, University of Alaska Archives)

at the Bank Saloon and the Pavillion and were wined and dined by the gold kings. A dance-hall girl was paid $125 a week and could make $25 a night in tips. "It was said that some girls made as high as $250 a night, but this could only be done by 'rolling,' which meant getting a man drunk and stealing his poke," Martha Black wrote. But like the gold kings, most of Dawson's good-time girls paid a heavy price, both physically and mentally, for the life they led.

A second fire during the night of April 26-27, 1899, wiped out the downtown, burning more than 100 buildings at a loss of more than $1 million. But it turned out to be a form of urban renewal. In place of the old log buildings, new buildings of finished lumber were built. Sewers were installed. Front Street was paved. If Dawson ever resembled Paris, it was after the fire.

But by July, Dawson's heyday was done.

Forces of Change

From the first gold strike, the forces of change had been mustering at Dawson. First were the North West Mounted Police. The Mounties — part army, part police force and part everything else — had been formed partly to deal with the Sioux Indians who, after teaching George Armstrong Custer his last lesson in warfare, had moved north into Canada. In the person of Inspector Charles Constantine, they had put in their first

The North West Mounted Police barracks housed about 30 constables, under the command of Inspector Charles Constantine, charged with maintaining law and order amid the chaos of gold-rush Dawson. According to Tappan Adney, the barracks consisted of eight or 10 log buildings, including officers' and men's quarters, court room, offices and post office. In addition to law enforcement, the Mounties handled the mail. (Photo by E.A. Hegg; P.E. Larss Collection, Alaska State Library)

appearance in the Yukon at Fortymile. After the Klondike strike, the Fortymile contingent established a barracks at Dawson under Inspector W.H. Scarth. Then, Inspector Sam Steele and his men came North to police the White and Chilkoot passes, taking the high ground and keeping Maxim guns handy in case there were any disputes about the customs duty. After shepherding the main part of the rush through Miles Canyon, Steele arrived in Dawson and took command of the barracks there.

Under Steele, the Mounties took a flexible approach to the law. They banned hand guns, obscenity, cheating and disorderly conduct. But they let the dance halls, saloons, gambling halls and cribs operate full tilt. Except on Sunday, when the town was shut down in observance of the Sabbath. Steele had the advantage of being his own justice of the peace and he sentenced malefactors to cut wood on the barracks woodpile. For more

serious infractions, he simply did what the miner's meetings had done: he exiled the lawbreaker, giving him a "blue ticket" out of the territory.

Law enforcement was only part of the Mounties' duties. "They carried mail and valuable shipments of gold between Dawson and Skagway . . ." wrote historian Melody Webb. "They looked after the indigent and the Indians. They served as game wardens, fire wardens, custom and tax collectors, coroners and justices of the peace. Most important, they controlled travel in and out of the Yukon."

The Mounties were not always as upright as the myths make them out to be; virtue was not easy for a constable making $1 a day while mine laborers were being paid $1.50 an hour. "It takes from three to five hours waiting in line to get to the door of the post office. . . . The Mounted Police turn an honest penny (?) by taking tips of 50¢ to $1 a letter

This photo of the Toronto Detachment of the Yukon Field Force was taken in Dawon at midnight, June 25, 1899. The 203-man force, organized by the Canadian government, was sent to the Klondike to prevent the predominantly American miners from annexing the Yukon to the United States.
(Photo by E.A. Hegg, Alaska State Library)

from those who do not care to wait so long," McMichael wrote. But newspaper editor Stroller White represented the prevailing view when he wrote: "In Dawson, also, the Royal North-West Mounted Police maintained a surprising degree of law and order considering the number of people congregated there and the kind of people many of them were."

The kind of people many — indeed, most — of them were was American, a fact that bothered the Canadian government no end. The gold seekers preferred their own laws and traditions and made few bones about it; the Fourth of July was for some years the most important holiday in Dawson. Now that the Yukon had some value, the government feared the Americans might seize the area by sheer weight of numbers. In the stampede summer of '98, the concern was so great that 200 Canadian soldiers were sent North as the Yukon Field Force. The force spent a year in the Yukon without firing a shot in anger, was dissolved, and its members went off to fight the Boer War in southern Africa.

Another of the civilizing forces was religion.

One of the most popular men of the cloth was Father William Judge, a Catholic missionary who had come over the frozen Yukon River from Fortymile during the winter of 1896-97 with such medical supplies as he had. Once in Dawson he opened both a church and a hospital. By the end of the gold rush summer his St. Mary's Hospital was full. Besides scurvy cases there were the malaria, typhoid and dysentery to be expected in a city built on a swamp. Judge's work with the sick was so selfless that, by the time he died in January 1899, he was being called "the Saint of Dawson."

Judge's church was one of five in Dawson, the others belonging to the Anglicans, Presbyterians, Methodists and Salvation

Army. There was no shortage of places for the miners to go when Steele closed down the town on Sundays.

Mainstream commerce had come to Dawson, too. By June 15, 1898, two banks, the Bank of British North America and the Canadian Bank of Commerce, had opened. The latter had imported paper money — special red bank notes with the words "Dawson" and "Yukon" printed onto them — and was paying from $15 to $17 an ounce for gold, depending on which creek it came from. Most of the old-timers scorned the "cheechako money," as they called it, but it was popular as souvenirs. Gold dust remained the coin of the realm; commercial dust, loaded with everything from sand to sawdust, was fixed at $11 an ounce.

In some ways, August 1898 is Dawson's watershed, the point at which the city began changing from boomtown to colonial outpost. Until the gold strike, the Yukon had been a part of the North West Territory, once called Rupert's Land. Since the Canadian government was concentrating its energies on settling its vast prairie, such attention as Ottawa paid to the North was cursory. But with the gold strike came incentives to make the Yukon a separate territory. It could provide some of its own revenue. Its government could provide jobs for supporters of the newly elected Liberal ruling party.

Limited self-government also offered a way to mollify the miners. That the miners were mostly Americans had moved the Canadian government to do more than just send troops. The miners were taking Canadian gold to U.S. businesses and mints, and the government meant to capture some of that wealth. So, in

1896, it changed its mining regulations to withhold alternating parcels of land for the government, taking potentially rich ground out from under the miners. A second provision was even less popular: it increased the royalty on gold to an effective rate of 20 percent in the Klondike fields. The miners responded with angry petitions. To avoid paying the royalty, they under-reported their take. All things considered, some conciliation seemed to be in order.

In August 1898 the Yukon was made a separate territory, with Dawson as its capital.

The same month, Arthur Newton Christian Treadgold left Dawson after a reconnaissance visit. Treadgold came away taken with the idea of controlling the Klondike goldfields. He saw his chance in the fact that the hand-miners were taking only the richest of the ore — a process called high-grading — because they didn't have the machinery to be more thorough. Whoever gained control of the machine mining that was to follow would control the Klondike.

Called "cheechako money," the Canadian Bank of Commerce imported special bank notes for circulation in the Klondike. Although old-timers scorned the notes and continued to pay their way with gold, the bank notes were at times a rarity and could be sold for more than their face value. (Courtesy of Canadian Imperial Bank of Commerce, reprinted from The Alaska Journal®)

The last, and by all accounts the most important, civilizing force was women; more precisely, wives.

Women had been a factor in the exploration and development of the North from the white man's arrival. Both the Russian-American and Hudson's Bay companies had encouraged their employees to marry native women, figuring a man with a native wife was much less likely to want to go home. The early miners often chose Indian wives, a decision that caused friction with the Indian men. "The Wolves (white men) have taken our women, and our men are childless. We are grown to a handful," says an Indian character

Workers show off their diggings on Adams Hill, above Bonanza Creek, in 1900. Note the tailing piles in the background. (Courtesy of Nicki Nielsen)

in Jack London's *The Son of the Wolf* (1981).

A few wives trickled into the North in the early years of mining. One of them, the wife of a miner named James Bean, was killed by the Indians in 1878. It wasn't until the founding of Circle City that any appreciable number of women began coming North, and most of them weren't wives. During the winter of 1897, Tappan Adney estimated there were about 200 women in Dawson.

But when the stampede hit Dawson the following summer, it contained, Adney wrote, "Australians with upturned sleeves and a swagger; young Englishmen in golf-stockings and tweeds; would-be miners in Mackinaws and rubber boots, or heavy, high-laced shoes; Japanese, negroes and women, too, everywhere."

These women, Martha Black wrote, belonged to three classes: "members of the oldest profession in the world, who ever followed armies and gold rushes; dance-hall and variety girls, whose business was to entertain and be dancing partners; and a few others, wives with unbounded faith in and love for their mates, or the odd person like myself on a special mission."

Women benefitted during the rush itself from the peculiar society that it created. "It is a great leveler — this Alaska country," McMichael wrote. "The merchant, millionaire, the ox pusher, mule driver and the ordinary individual who sleds his own outfit over the pass have the same rough and tough appearance." This leveling, mentioned in most writing of the time, gave women a lot of freedom. "A significant outgrowth of this special social milieu was that relationships between men and women flourished with few of the formalities and inhibitions generally associated with the late Victorian era," wrote modern commentator Laurie Alberts.

This was not to be true for long in Dawson City. Changes in the year between the summers of 1898 and 1899 made Dawson much easier to reach and much more pleasant to live in. The first of the changes was the shooting of Soapy Smith in Skagway in July 1898. The town's merchants had decided Smith's crimes were bad for business. They formed a vigilante group and moved to oust him. When he tried to crash one of their indignation meetings, a surveyor named Frank Reid shot him dead. Skagway quickly became much more law-abiding.

It also became the head of a railroad into the Yukon. The White Pass and Yukon Railroad was begun in April 1898. By July of the following year, it had reached Lake Bennett. The railroad became part of the transportation network that included a large number of steamboats, operated by several companies, that plied the waters between St. Michael and Whitehorse. Their size and number allowed more goods and passengers to be carried, lowering costs and increasing the kinds of goods for sale in Dawson. These changes occurred so quickly that, when Martha Black went Outside in August 1899, she took a steamboat to Whitehorse, a tram around the rapids, a river steamer to Lake Bennett and the railroad to Skagway. Walking was no longer required. Wives and families could be brought in from the south to live, if only for the summers. And with them would come a tamer way of life.

The Rush Ends

Each of these forces exerted a civilizing influence on Dawson. But the event that allowed them to get the upper hand was the news of a big, new strike at Nome.

Many of the men who lived in Dawson during the winter of 1898-99 were not thriving. Those who prospected the creeks found little of value. Those who worked on other men's claims or in Dawson's businesses earned just enough to get by. Many did nothing at all. They were spectators at the feast. When summer arrived many of them

Winter transportation was available between Dawson and Whitehorse on the White Pass and Yukon Route stage line. Although the stage route did not follow the river and thus cut about 70 miles off the distance between the two towns, the trip took five days or more, depending on weather.
(Courtesy of Nicki Nielsen)

gave up and began heading south. But others heard rumors of the Nome strike and stayed until midsummer, when the rumors were confirmed. Then they stampeded. Most of them would be too late there, too, but they didn't know that.

With them went many of Dawson's gaudiest entrepreneurs. Arizona Charlie Meadows had just finished work on his Palace Grand Theater, a plush and mammoth showplace on King Street built of lumber salvaged from two steamers. Now that it was unlikely to be profitable, he proposed to float it to Nome. Instead, he left it behind. Sam Bonnifield, high-stakes gambler and owner of the Bank Saloon, went to Nome and then Fairbanks, where he opened a real bank and had a street named after him. In Nome Tex Rickard made the money to open the Madison Square Garden in New York, where he promoted fights just as he had in Wyatt Earp's Nome saloon.

Tom Lippy had returned to Dawson that June to take more than a quarter of a million dollars home from No. 16 Eldorado. The

Arizona Charlie Meadows promised Dawson residents that his Palace Grand Theater would be the most lavish dance hall the town had ever seen. The theater opened in 1899 with a production of Camille. By this time, however, Dawson was in decline and Meadows soon left for the new diggings at Nome. (University of Alaska Archives, reprinted from The Alaska Journal®)

Reverend Edward M. Randall, who accompanied him, found Dawson "a city of fully 20,000, unique in history, wealth and wickedness." Before the pair got back to Seattle with the gold, that description was out of date. In August alone, according to Pierre Berton, 8,000 people left Dawson bound for Nome. In the summer of '99, the golden path led straight out of town.

The Nome stampede took the boom out of Dawson, but the town remained a lively and vital place. As Lippy's cleanup showed, there was still gold to be mined. In fact, reported gold production rose to $16 million in 1899. How much of that was because the government royalty had been halved is anybody's guess. Supplying the creeks and entertaining the miners provided a steady business for Dawson. The government provided more jobs. The Yukon's first public road, between Dawson and the creeks, was built that year.

But the end of the old, labor-intensive hand mining was in sight. On the Stewart River's Cassiar Bar, a dredge was at work, scraping the bedrock and sorting the gold from the gravel. The Klondike was next.

An image of George Carmack adorns the cover of the only edition of the Klondike News *ever published. For a fee, Arizona Charlie Meadows included in it the stories of miners who had struck it rich. The single issue raised about $50,000 for Meadows. (University of Washington Library, reprinted from* The Alaska Journal®)

Promoters and Capitalists

By the 1901 census, Dawson's population was down to 9,142. As the census taker canvassed the town that summer, big changes were occurring. The last Klondike staking rush was over. The government, anxious to stimulate the sagging economy, had opened some of its Eldorado Creek claims the previous winter. A new paystreak was unearthed, but the increased production did not offset declines in other mines. Gold production for the year was $20 million, $4 million less than in 1900.

With an eye toward the end of hand mining, the government had begun to issue concessions, or leases. These concessions granted the right to mine large pieces of

This bird's-eye view of the Klondike River valley shows mining activity from the river's mouth (at the extreme lower left) to Bear Creek. (Photo by J. Doody, courtesy of Mrs. James Doogan)

ground. The theory behind them was that the mining of low-grade ore would be profitable only if done mechanically and over much larger areas than the hand miners were allowed to claim.

Treadgold was maneuvering for a concession. He wanted the rights to mine the entire Klondike drainage. In return, he offered a scheme to supply the water necessary to carry out large-scale mining operations. Treadgold's plan highlighted the difference between machine and hand mining; the former required a lot of money. The machines had to be built and shipped north. The power plants to run them had to be bought, water had to be brought in. Where hand mining was labor intensive, machine mining was capital intensive. Treadgold had commitments for the money from associates in London. If he succeeded in getting his concession, there were going to be a lot fewer jobs in the Klondike goldfields.

Money could provide everything but the ground to work. Under Canadian law, that ground was supposed to be not suitable for placer mining and certified as such by government officials at Dawson. To grant the concessions, then, the government was going to have to state that some of the richest gold-producing acreage in the world could not be mined by hand.

The first Klondike concession had been given to Robert Anderson of London. Anderson had claimed the land he proposed to mine hydraulically was too poor to mine profitably by hand. In 1897, he was given the lease, with certain conditions, for two-and-a-half miles of Hunker Creek.

Another concession had been issued in 1900 to Joe Boyle. Boyle was a former prospector and fight promoter who had come to Dawson during the rush with Frank Slavin, a former heavyweight champion of Canada. The Boyle Concession, called Lease No. 18,

One of the attractions at Bear Creek is Joe Boyle's house (right), built about 1904. Along with former Australian heavyweight boxer Frank Slavin, Boyle reached Dawson in August 1897 with $19 and a bare-bones mining outfit. From 1907 until 1916 he owned the Canadian Klondyke Mining Company and was the dominant force in Dawson mining circles. To the left of Boyle's house is the single secretaries' residence, where unmarried women working at Bear Creek were required to live. (Mike Doogan)

covered about 40 square miles of the Klondike River valley between the mouths of Hunker and Bonanza creeks.

In 1901, Treadgold finally got his concession. He and his British backers were given control of the portion of the goldfield lying in the Klondike River watershed, including all of Bonanza, Eldorado, Bear and Hunker creeks, with the exception of existing claims and water rights.

The miners in Dawson reacted angrily to these concessions which they saw, quite rightly, as a threat to their claims and ability to make a living. They held indignation meetings and drafted petitions requesting the concessions be cancelled.

The miners disliked both the law and the people who ran the government, an opinion that had prevailed since the first mining in the Klondike. "If there were not serious disorders it was due less to the quality of government than to the orderly character of the population," Adney wrote. Flora Shaw, a correspondent for *The Times* of London was, in a report from Dawson in September 1898, even blunter: "To put the position as plainly as it is daily and hourly stated in the mining fields and in the steets of Dawson, there is a widely prevalent conviction not only that the laws are bad, but that the officers through which they are administered are corrupt."

To quell the 1898 unrest, the man in charge of the Yukon for the federal government, Minister of the Interior Clifford Sifton, called on none other than William Ogilvie. Ogilvie, recently appointed Commissioner of the Yukon, was as honest as the northern summer day was long, and the miners knew it. Sifton named him to head an inquiry into charges of favoritism in the granting of claims and other government malfeasance. Ogilvie muddled through without finding any evidence to support the charges or convincing the miners they were false.

Although the concessions sparked controversy — and were modified, changed, revoked, reinstituted and wrangled over during the next 40 years — they were the sure signs that Klondike mining was changed.

Another sure sign, if one was needed, was the arrival of the first dredge. This was the so-called Discovery Dredge, moved from the Stewart River to Bonanza Creek in 1901 by the Lewes River Mining and Dredging Company. It was small by the standards of the dredges that would follow, with its three-and-one-quarter cubic foot buckets, but it was a significant advance in mining technology nonetheless.

The dredge was essentially a boat full of

Steam shovel Number 2, the "Little Giant," works on Yukon Gold Company's Twelvemile Ditch in August 1906. The ditch, completed in 1911, carried water from the Little Twelvemile River, first to a power plant, then 70 miles to the goldfields. (Public Archives of Canada/PA-102885, reprinted from The Gold Hustlers *[1977])*

mining equipment. It floated in a pond created by digging a pit around the dredge and then flooding it. The dredge was anchored by a big hunk of metal called a spud. On the front of the dredge was the bucket line. The buckets dug up gravel and rocks and carried them inside the dredge, where they were washed and rotated to separate the gold. The rocks and gravel were then conveyed out the rear of the dredge and stacked in tailing piles. Since the dredge pivoted on the spud as it worked, the tailing piles it left behind were curved. When the dredge buckets had gobbled up all the gravel within reach, the spud was lifted, the dredge winched forward along lines attached to land, and the spud dropped. In this way, the dredge carried its own pond with it.

Gold production dropped again in 1902, to $13 million, as more and more of the easily accessible high-grade ore was mined out. The mining regulations were changed to allow the working of a number of claims in partnership, and the old-style hand miner was doomed. Many of them began to leave the country that year; early the next, others joined the latest rush and went to Fairbanks.

As the amount of ground necessary to make mining pay grew, the methods of mining changed. If the creek bottoms were to be the reserve of the dredges, the benches would require hydraulic monitors. The monitors, or giants as they were sometimes known, were high-pressure nozzles that focused the force of water on the hillside, stripping away the overburden and washing the gravel down to sluices. With enough water pressure, one man with a monitor could do the work of dozens without. The need for water is what caused much of the

A 40-ton dredge spud lies rusting near Bear Creek. The spud was a large pin around which a working dredge pivoted by means of a winch connected to anchors on shore.
(Mike Doogan)

opposition to the Treadgold Concession, because it gave him what amounted to a water monopoly in the goldfields.

In 1903, continued complaints about the concessions, particularly Treadgold's, finally forced the government to appoint yet another commission. Known as the Britton Commission, it took testimony in Dawson on the concessions, much of it embarrassing to the government. Finally, by June 1904, the heat generated by the opposition proved too much for Sifton, some of whose friends held other concessions that were under attack. He cancelled the Treadgold Concession. This did not stop Treadgold, who continued to scheme to control the goldfields.

But Joe Boyle, who had managed to retain his concession, got started first. Boyle for some time had been looking around for backers with the money to pay for mining his concession. About the time Treadgold lost his concession, Boyle was negotiating with a Detroit branch of the Rothschild family and their company, the Detroit Yukon Mining Company. Together, they formed the Canadian Klondyke Mining Company and made plans to mine the Klondike valley.

The formation of Canadian Klondyke accomplished several things. It guaranteed that there would be a future for Yukon mining. It opened the way for large-scale dredging. It saved Boyle's financial bacon; at the time of the agreement, he was not living up to the terms of the lease and was being sued for debt by several parties. It also, in a roundabout way, helped set a Stanley Cup hockey record.

This was vintage Joe Boyle. While on his way to negotiate with the Rothschilds in

Workers assemble redwood stave pipe on the Lepine Ridge section of the Twelvemile Ditch in 1907. Along its 70-mile length it was ditch, open flume, redwood stave pipe and, where the pressure was greatest, steel pipe. (Public Archives of Canada/PA-103035, reprinted from The Gold Hustlers *[1977])*

Detroit, he had stopped in Ottawa to attend to various matters. While there, he bragged that a hockey team from Yukon could win the Stanley Cup, the symbol of supremacy in the sport. Then as now, Yukon was not a hotbed of hockey activity. Its population was small and, all too often, its severe cold limited winter play outdoors. But Boyle, who was nothing if not flamboyant, put a team together anyway. It was drawn mainly from Dawson, still the territory's largest city, and contained a heavy salting of Mounties. January 1905 found it, with manager Joe Boyle, in Ottawa to play for the cup. The Yukoners lost the first game of the playoff to the Ottawa Silver Seven, 9 to 2. In the second game, the Yukoners again scored two goals. But the Ottawa team netted 23, for a margin of victory unsurpassed in Stanley Cup play.

Boyle was more successful at mining. In August 1905 his company put Rothschild No. 1, later to be renamed Canadian No. 1, into operation on Bear Creek. The dredge was a behemoth: it weighed 500 tons; its hull was 100 feet long and 28 feet wide; each of its buckets would hold seven cubic feet of material. It was powered by its own wood-fired power plant. For the next 33 years it would work the Klondike creeks.

Treadgold countered the following year. In March 1906 a party of engineers arrived at

Dawson and began laying plans for a ditch to carry water from the Little Twelvemile River, first to a power plant, then 70 miles to the goldfields. This ambitious project showed that Treadgold, too, had found some real money. His backers were the Guggenheims, the premier U.S. mining family. Clearly, the promoter and the capitalist had taken over the goldfields.

By 1907, the power plant was in operation, and three dredges were working for the

This undated photo shows Dawson City's Champion Hockey Team, perhaps the Yukoners, which Joe Boyle organized in 1904 to compete for the Stanley Cup. In January 1905 the team was soundly defeated by the Ottawa Silver Seven. (MacBride Museum Photo Collection)

Treadgold-Guggenheim company, called the Yukon Gold Company. More dredges followed, put into operation by both Yukon

The first electrically operated dredge in the Klondike was Rothschild No. 1 (later renamed Canadian No. 1), shown here at work on Bear Creek in 1906. The Rothschild family of Detroit, who at that time controlled the Canadian Klondyke Mining Company and the Boyle Concession, financed the dredge. (Yukon Archives, J. Doody Collection; reprinted from The Gold Hustlers [1977])

With Joe Boyle's voracious Canadian No. 4 looming in the background, a group of men meets for a final photo in front of the Old Inn just before the building was to be dredged out on June 29, 1913. The inn was saved temporarily when it was discovered that the Yukon Gold Company, rival of Boyle's Canadian Klondyke Mining Company, controlled the land it was on. (Yukon Archives, MacBride Museum Collection; reprinted from The Gold Hustlers [1977])

Gold and Canadian Klondyke. In 1911, Yukon Gold's engineers finished the Yukon's most amazing engineering feat, the 70-mile ditch to bring water to the Klondike valley. Along its length it was ditch, open flume, redwood stave pipe and, where the pressure was greatest, steel pipe.

Gold production had continued to decline until 1908, when it hit $3.3 million. The years immediately following were relatively stable: $4 million in 1909, $4.6 million in 1910; $4.6 million again in 1911.

By that year, Boyle had maneuvered his way through a maze of contracts and lawsuits and come out sole owner of Canadian Klondyke. Treadgold had split with the Guggs, as they were known in the goldfields, but had not given up plotting. The companies were mining gold and, although their books made it difficult to tell how much — if any — money they were making, at least men were working. Dawson was not faring quite so well. In 1911, her population was 3,013. The city had shrunk by two-thirds in 10 years.

This view shows two dredges, Canadian No. 3 and Canadian No. 4, being built at the Canadian Klondyke Mining Company construction camp at Bonanza Basin in 1912. In the right background is Yukon Gold Company's "Guggieville," so-called because of the Guggenheim family's interest in the company. (Courtesy of Mrs. James Doogan)

Third annual picnic of the M.E.
of Dawson, Y.T.
Aug. 1901.   Photo By Mrs G

Dawson Society

In much the same way as a dredge carried its own pond, the post-rush arrivals carried their own society with them. In 1901, Dawson was still a mining town, but it was no longer dominated by the mining society. There were more than 1,000 women, mostly wives and mothers, living in Dawson, as well as a number of government employees. Around the territorial commissioner a sort of colonial administration society grew up. It was modeled, not surprisingly, on the society created throughout the world by British bureaucrats. Also not surprisingly, the bureaucrats occupied the society's highest positions.

The wives and bureaucrats began to spruce up Dawson. The prostitutes who remained in

A group of children enjoys the fresh air during its third annual Sunday school picnic in August 1901. (Bassoc Collection, University of Alaska Archives)

Paradise Alley were banished across the Klondike River to Lousetown. Gambling was outlawed, and liquor and dance-hall regulations were changed to eliminate, for all practical purposes, the hurdy-gurdy girls' livelihood. Government undercover agents were paid to expose women of loose virtue. Women of the better element formed committees to keep their social inferiors from attending their soirees.

One of the people put out of business by this outbreak of morality was Klondike Kate Rockwell. In the 1920s and 1930s she would be known, mainly from stories in the Outside press, as one of the gold rush's queens. In fact, Rockwell got to Dawson in 1900. But she did well for herself once there, posing as a teenager and earning as much as $750 a night singing, dancing and roller skating around the stage in pink tights. She took as her lover a Greek bartender named Alex Pantages and together they bought the Palace Grand, by

then called the Orpheum. But the new regulations cut the theater's profits and, unable to make a go of what the law allowed, the pair left. Pantages used Kate's money to start a theater chain that became the largest in the U.S., then dumped her.

In response to the increasing number of families in Dawson and the outlying settlements, the Yukon government took the first decennial census and used it as the basis for building five schools for the 175 children it found in Dawson. The schoolteachers the government hired got the same $150 a month paid to territorial firemen and doctors.

Despite this and other social expenditures, the official government policy was to limit spending in the North. Ottawa's bureaucrats doubted the area would support significant sustained economic activity or many people. Because of this, and the low wages paid by the government, officials had often held simultaneous jobs with the federal and ter-

Dawson employees of the North American Trading and Transportation Company show off their costumes before participating in the Fourth of July parade in 1900. (Photo by Larss & Duclos; P.E. Larss Collection, Alaska State Library)

ritorial governments. This served to reinforce the territory's lack of status, while at the same time keeping down the number of government-paid wage-earners. As the population shrank, so did the number of government jobs.

For awhile, private spending offset government thrift. The White Pass and Yukon Route Railway had expanded into running steamers on the river, resulting in lower freight costs. The plants that powered the dredges also provided electricity to the city. There was private telephone service, a winter stage line (also run by the White Pass and Yukon) and fire-fighting equipment bought by the citizens.

But what Dawson gained on the corners, she lost on the roundabouts. Martha Black, by now remarried to Yukon lawyer and politician George Black, wrote of Dawson society: "There were teas, receptions, dinner and card parties, and dances, and I must not forget the amateur plays." She wrote of the club activities, summer boating, camping and hunting and the occasional visit by some dignitary. This was a far cry from the gold kings and hurdy-gurdy girls. With her population went much of Dawson's vitality. The card party replaced the card game.

Contestants take a break during the Dawson Curling Club Championship game between J.T. Lithgow and Colonel Rourke, April 9, 1901. (University of Alaska Archives)

A group of children, bundled against the cold, stands with its teacher in front of one of five schools built in Dawson in 1901. In response to the increasing number of families in town and in the outlying settlements, the Yukon government took its first decennial census in that year and used it as the basis for building schools for the 175 children it found in the area. (University of Washington Historical Photograph Collection, reprinted from The Alaskan Gold Fields [1983])

The best chronicler of Dawson descending was Laura Berton, who traveled to the Yukon in 1907 to take one of the teaching jobs (by then the salary had shot up to $175 a month). There she found, and described, a society rigid with rules and steeped in irony. The bedrock of that society was the "day" every proper woman was expected to give each month, during which she was at home to her peers. The success of these days, and the importance of their givers, was measured by how many people attended. "Thus it was possible to compute the social standing of the entire upper crust of Dawson City mathematically," she wrote. As a teacher, Berton had a place below the salt, but a place. She, too, went to endless parties and teas and ". . . *bals poudres,* when the entire town turned out in powdered wigs and eighteenth-century costumes to emulate the court of Versailles, so, many leagues and so many years distant from the Arctic Brotherhood Hall in Dawson City."

Berton saw just as clearly the cause of all this posturing: the decline of the city and the boredom of its residents. In concrete terms, that decline meant not just fantastic costumes and precise social scales but that "There was no problem about finding a house to rent cheaply in Dawson. Meat and butter might

Ornate Victorian scrollwork adorns Dawson's Government House, official residence of the commissioner of Yukon Territory. The house burned in 1906 and was remodeled in a much simpler style. (Yukon Archives, Alaska Historical Library Collection; reprinted from Martha Black *[1986])*

ABOVE—*Nurses staff the "Palace of Sweets" at the St. Mary's Hospital Fair, held in the Palace Grand Theater around 1900. Dawson residents turned out in large numbers for elaborately decorated affairs such as this. (Photo by Larss & Duclos; P.E. Larss Collection, Alaska State Library)*

LEFT—*Poet Robert Service, one of Dawson's best-known residents, was a nondescript Englishman who had been educated in Scotland. He worked for the Canadian Bank of Commerce in Vancouver and Whitehorse, and came to the Dawson branch in 1908. (Yukon Archives, Gillis Collection; reprinted from* The Alaska Journal®*)*

be selling for double the accepted price, but homes were a drug on the market."

The year after Berton arrived, a new employee for the city's Canadian Bank of Commerce branch reached Dawson. He was a nondescript Englishman who had been educated in Scotland and had knocked around the world some until, in 1903, he hired on at the bank's Vancouver office. In the fall of 1904, he was sent to work at the Whitehorse branch. His name was Robert Service.

Ironically, Service wrote most of his best-known verse about the Klondike before he ever laid eyes on Dawson City. He got started in Whitehorse when Stroller White suggested he write something for a church concert. That something turned out to be *The Shooting of Dan McGrew,* which was declared too raw for the concert. But Service kept writing and eventually sent a manuscript off to a publisher along with $100 to defray printing costs. The publisher returned the $100 but printed *Songs of a Sourdough* (published in the U.S. as *The Spell of the Yukon*) in 1907. It was a smash; 24 editions had been printed by 1912. In 1908, the bank sent Service to Dawson, where he worked in the branch and continued to write verse. He quit the bank in 1909 to work on his only novel, *The Trail of '98* (1910).

In a newspaper interview shortly after his arrival in Dawson, Service had declared himself disappointed in the town: "I find more empty places and more small cabins. I had learned to picture it in my mind as really greater."

Dawson was not "really greater," but it was surviving. The town had become a supply center for the creek mining operations, a rest and recreation center for miners from the goldfields and a government service center. As the largest city for some distance along the area's most-traveled river, Dawson also drew people from up and down the Yukon, come to town for shopping and maybe a little spree. The city was surviving, but shrinking. The Blacks left in 1909, George to take the British Columbia bar exam. They were to return several years later. In 1912, Service left for the last time, taking the fortune he'd made from mining the Klondike in his own way and

The Dawson Aerie No. 50 of the Fraternal Order of Eagles decorated the Arctic Brotherhood Hall in honor of the 10th anniversary of the order's founding, February 6, 1908. (Photo by Duclos; P.E. Larss Collection, Alaska State Library)

moving to France. The same year, the NAT&T closed its Dawson store. Of 1912, Berton wrote, "There were now not more than two thousand people left in town, and fewer than that in the winter."

War and Depression

The passing years had been hard on Dawson, but they'd been good to Joe Boyle. He'd spent them suing and being sued, and he came out of court in 1911 with full control of the Canadian Klondyke Mining Company. As the man on top of one of the biggest companies in the goldfields, he was "King of the Klondike." In 1913, he drove a visiting party from the International Geological Congress around the creeks in his auto, showing them, in the words of H.M. Cadell, "great hospitality." Cadell was not as impressed with the town: "At the time of my visit Dawson City had a population of only 2,000, and the place was in a sorry condition, while the surrounding district was almost depleted of drift miners."

He might be only the biggest fish in an evaporating pond, but Boyle was still a compelling figure. "A man of iron build, good-looking, a dominant personality, he was welcomed everywhere," Martha Black wrote.

" 'Tis true he was quarrelsome, overbearing and intolerant, determined to the point of obstinacy in business dealings. . . ." Because he lived at the company's Bear Creek camp, Boyle was not a full member of the Dawson social set, called by then the Ping-Pongs, as were the officials of his main competitors, Yukon Gold.

In 1913, his company put two more dredges into operation; with their 16-foot buckets, they were the largest in the Klondike. Boyle drove around his holdings in his Flanders 20 and every summer gave a party for the children of Dawson. But when war broke out in Europe, the Yukon couldn't hold him for long.

The first thing he did was organize the Boyle Yukon Machine Gun Detachment, 50 men from the Yukon financed by Joe Boyle. They went off to fight without Boyle, who was considered too old to serve. Once in the army, the detachment was broken up and members

spread around the Canadian Army, where they served with much distinction. Boyle stayed behind for two years, his company failing financially and embroiled in lawsuits. By 1916, he couldn't stand it any longer and slipped off to Europe. A few months later he was followed by George Black, who was Yukon commissioner. Black resigned, organized the Yukon Infantry Company with himself as captain, and went off to fight the war.

Martha Black went with him and, in London in 1918, met up with Boyle again. He had been put to work organizing British transportation in the Moscow area, she wrote, and following the Bolshevik Revolution, had spirited the Romanian treasury back to Romania. The country was cut off, but Boyle managed to get supplies into it. "Undoubtedly but for him Romania would have starved, and his deeds were considered by both the Romanian and British governments as miraculous," Black wrote. Boyle became the "Savior of Romania." He never returned to Dawson.

During the war, as more and more young men went off to fight, gold production plunged to half of its prewar level. Dawson's population continued to shrink. The cessation of hostilities did not restore it. Laura Berton's husband, Frank, had also gone off to fight and by the time the couple returned to Dawson in 1921, the population was less than 1,000. During the winter it was even fewer. The decennial census was taken in summer, and estimates are that from one-fourth to one-half of the summer residents wintered elsewhere. "The last boat was always packed with the wealthy going out for the winter, the fortunate going out forever, and the sick going out to die," Berton wrote.

In 1918, none of them made it. One hundred and twenty-five of Dawson's rich, fortunate and sick were among the 343 passengers and crew aboard the *Princess Sophia* when she left Skagway for Vancouver. The weather was stormy, and the ship ran aground. For a night and a day other ships stood by to remove her passengers but the captain refused to evacuate. The second night, October 25, the hull, pounded against the reef by the storm, split. All aboard were lost. It was the deadliest shipping disaster ever on the West Coast, and a calamity for Dawson and the Yukon. "The loss of so many friends and business leaders was a harsh blow for a territory already ravaged by the social costs of a distant war," wrote historian Kenneth Coates. "There was hardly a family not hit in some way," Berton wrote. "The Yukon Gold Company, the Northern Commercial,

A freight train of the Klondike Mines Railway carries a load of lumber from Dawson to Sulphur Springs, along Bonanza Creek. Construction of the railway was completed in 1906 and it operated until 1914. (University of Washington Collection, Yukon Archives; courtesy of Nicki Nielsen)

the government service, the steamboats, all were shattered by the wreck of the *Sophia.*

Because of the financial shenanigans of Boyle and Treadgold, the goldfields were in bad shape, too. With Boyle gone, Treadgold managed in 1923 to form yet another company — called the Yukon Consolidated Gold Corporation Limited (YCGC) — and began acquiring other companies working in the goldfields. By 1929, this consolidation was complete. But Treadgold never had enough, or made enough, money to pay off his debts. Nor did he limit his spending. His creditors got together to oust him in 1930, although litigation surrounding both the consolidation and the ouster continued for some time.

The new owners of YCGC managed to keep the company operating, although it wasn't easy. In 1930, they had to personally guarantee the cost of supplies and ask the workers to defer their salaries. But they squeezed every nickel, and at the end of the next year they were operating in the black. Gold production in 1931 yielded nearly three-quarters of a million dollars, with more than $100,000 left after debts were paid. The following year, the company's gold revenue fell to $685,000 but by then YCGC was on sounder financial footing.

"In Dawson, shrunken by war and disaster

and old age, the prewar pattern of social life went on, though on a smaller scale," Berton wrote. There were no longer enough people left in the town to allow for much social stratification. Women were allowed into the International Order of Daughters of the Empire, the town's most exclusive club, "whether they were, in the words of the national regent, 'the best people' or not," wrote Berton.

It was an odd society. Women still had their "days," but the daughters of the better class were allowed to date Mounties. The dancers at the balls twirled in the intricate rhythym of the minuet, but from time to time the mothers would vanish to the cloakroom to check their babies. Milk from the town's only cows arrived in whisky bottles, water in

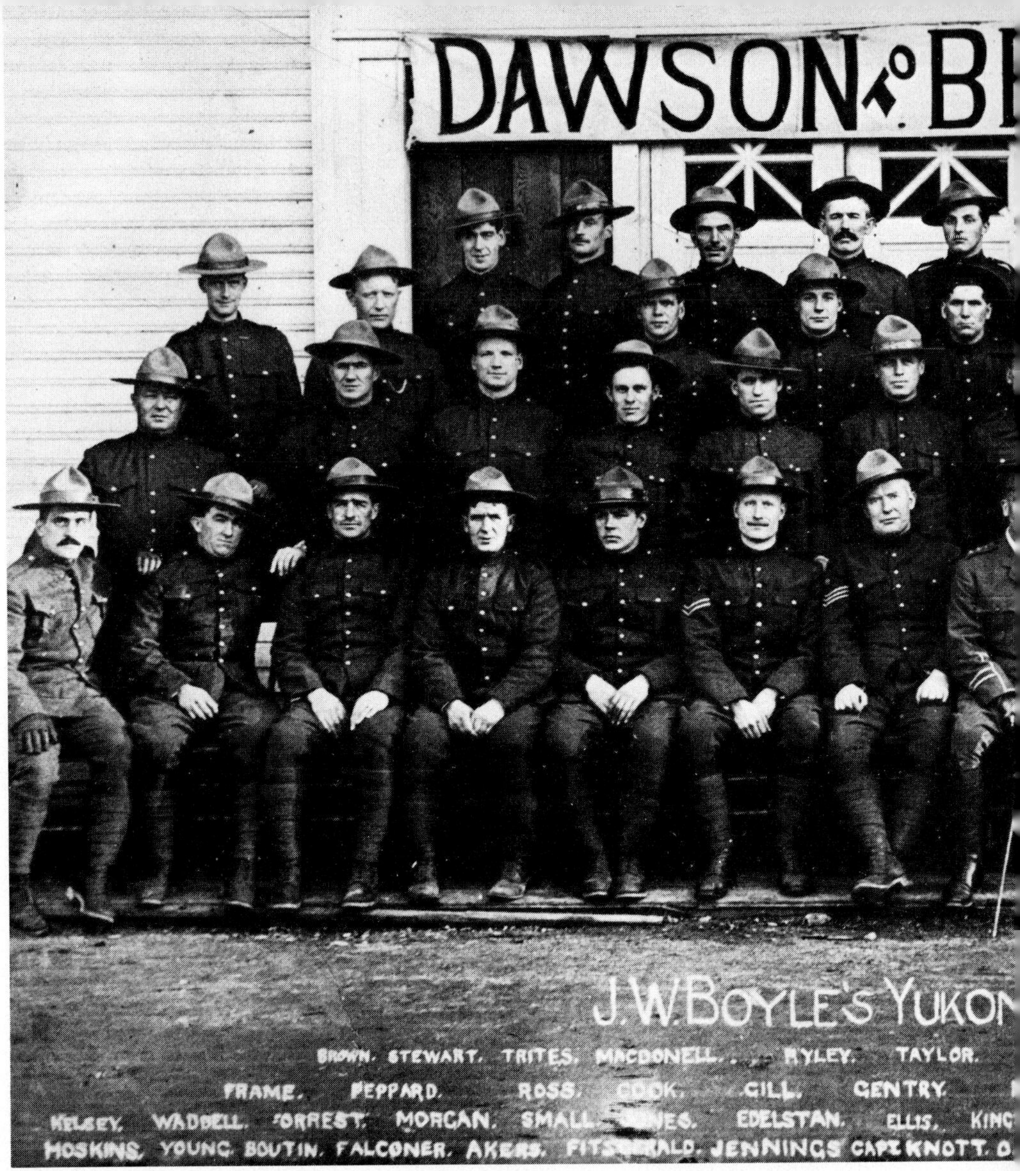

Prominent resident Joe Boyle was always active in Dawson community affairs. In 1913 Boyle began the annual ritual of taking all the town's children on a picnic, which he reportedly enjoyed as much as the youngsters did. (Yukon Archives, Martha Black Collection; reprinted from The Gold Hustlers *[1977])*

gasoline tins hauled by the town waterman. All through the '20s Dawson hung on to such of its traditions as its residents had the strength and numbers to maintain. Outside, flappers danced the Charleston and speakeasies thrived. In Dawson, which along with the rest of the Yukon had narrowly rejected prohibition, the engraved calling cards continued to accumulate on silver trays.

Increasingly, the town's residents began to see tourists. In the summer, the steamboats would bring people to see what remained of the great gold rush metropolis, to watch gold being mined and to gawk at Robert Service's

In 1914 Joe Boyle organized and financed the Yukon Machine Gun Detachment, 50 men from the Yukon who went off to fight in World War I. The unit became one of the most decorated in the Canadian Army. (Yukon Archives, MacBride Museum Collection; reprinted from The Gold Hustlers *[1977])*

With money from the tourists and the goldfields, Dawson hung on into the 1930s. But the decline continued. In 1931, the census found a population of 819. Then the Great Depression, of all things, intervened in Dawson's favor. Work in the goldfields was not pleasant. Nor did it pay well. But there was work. So Dawson was spared the dislocation and despair of the Depression. In 1933, the YCGC produced more than $1 million in gold; in 1934, just less than that amount. The following year, the company began building new dredges. Dawson was on the uptick.

But the Yukon, with a population of barely more than 4,000 in 1931, continued to be a financial burden to the federal government. So Ottawa was receptive to an idea put forward by British Columbia Premier Duff Pattullo to annex the territory. Pattullo had been in Dawson during the rush, and thought that coupling the mineral rich Yukon to his province would enhance the development of both. The Yukoners resisted, and the question of continued funding for Dawson's Catholic school broke the back of Pattullo's plan.

By 1939, when YCGC produced $2.7 million in gold, more than 500 men and 10 dredges were working in the Klondike goldfields. Dawson's population was inching upward, and there was reason to think the worst was over. Then the city nearly became a casualty of war.

cabin. They were following in the footsteps of not only the many stampeders who were inadvertent tourists, but also the rush's first official sightseers. In the summer of '98, Edith Van Buren, niece of the former U.S. president, and a widow named Mary Hitchcock had arrived with exotic foods, pets and a collection of oddments that amazed even the bizarre denizens of Dawson. They held court in a big tent for awhile, then boarded a steamer to continue their tour. Their successors helped keep the hotels and restaurants of the much-shunken Dawson open.

War and Peace

One of the men working in the Yukon in 1939 was a 24-year-old named Jim Doogan. Like many of the workers, he was American, on summer vacation from the university at Fairbanks. He was cleaning up old claims on Clear Creek, not far from where Big Alex McDonald had died 30 years before. Among other things, he burned old sluice boxes and then recovered the gold from the ashes by using mercury. When he got to Dawson on supply runs, he would stop and drink coffee at a cafe run by a woman who had worked the dance halls during the rush.

Then, in September, England went to war and Canada went with her. Doogan returned to Alaska standing in the back of a flatbed truck as it pounded over the tractor road that

ran from Dawson across the border. Before the war was over there would be a much better road. It would nearly kill Dawson.

U.S. military planners had intended for some time to build a highway across Canada to link Alaska with the rest of the nation. But the Canadian government stuck to its policy of minimal northern investment and refused to allow the road to go forward. The Japanese invasion of the Aleutians made the road a military priority and, on the theory that defense of Alaska was defense of Canada, the Canadians gave in. A pioneer road, stretching from Edmonton to Fairbanks, was completed by the end of 1942 and a so-called all-weather road the following year. The Alcan Highway was no mean engineering feat, and it was to be a force for change in the North. But it didn't run through Dawson City.

The planners had had to consider supplying the road builders, so the highway route ran between supply points. Whitehorse was

one, because supplies for the highway could be landed at Skagway and brought to Whitehorse by the railroad. In the same way another military project, a string of airports to connect Edmonton and Fairbanks called the Northwest Staging Route, also went through Whitehorse instead of Dawson. The latter had an airfield, about 12 miles out of town, but the one at Whitehorse was considered superior.

The Alcan, now called the Alaska Highway, turned out to be of dubious military value. But it did provide a faster means of transportation than the old river routes, and it became a channel along which development flowed.

The war cut into both the population of Dawson and the production of the goldfields. In 1941 the census found just more than 1,000 residents in Dawson, but that number soon began dropping as more and more young men went off to fight. Likewise, as the number of laborers for the goldfields decreased, so did gold production. YCGC required about 700 workers to operate at full capacity. In 1942, the number of workers averaged 400 and production was $2.8 million; two years later, those numbers were 172 and $616,000.

After the war, the situation for both YCGC and Dawson changed substantially. At first, the company's production rose again. But the cheap labor that had been the bedrock of its financial success was no longer available. In addition, its equipment was wearing out and was too expensive to replace. The fixed price of gold, $35 an ounce, did not yield enough profit to justify adding new ground to be worked or buying new equipment. The company kept working through the 1950s, but the end of operations was in sight.

In 1951, Dawson's population was 783, an all-time low. So was its importance in the ter-

The steamer Keno, *shown here in 1943, plied the Yukon River for many years, bringing supplies to Dawson and other communities along the river. Now dry-docked, the ship is a popular tourist attraction.*
(Steve McCutcheon)

Sternwheelers are tied up behind barges loaded with U.S. Army vehicles at the Dawson City dock in 1942. (Haines Collection, Yukon Archives)

ritory. In 1921, for example, Dawson's population of 975 was about one-quarter of the Yukon's. But her 1951 population was only 8.5 percent of the territory's. In the 10 years between 1941 and 1951, while Dawson's population declined by about 250, the Yukon's nearly doubled. Because of her road and rail links, Whitehorse got most of that population and most of the benefits of the economic activity. Whitehorse had become the dominant city in the territory.

Official recognition of this came in 1951, when the decision was made to move the seat of the territorial government from Dawson to Whitehorse. The move was finished in 1953, taking with it more steady jobs. The same year the Klondike Loop Highway was pushed through to Dawson, tying it to the road system. Even after Dawson had started to decline, steamboats continued to haul supplies to, and ore from, Dawson. They also served other mining communities. But the

roads replaced the rivers as the routes for travelers and freight. Between 1941 and 1955, the number of annual trips by riverboats from Whitehorse to Dawson shrank from 51 to 10. Part of Dawson's decline had come with this shift; it was a central river town but a peripheral road town.

What many thought would be the final blow came in 1966, when YCGC shut down. The company had already stopped trading with the town, opening a commissary at Bear Creek. And, increasingly, its workers had come and gone without doing much business in Dawson. But the shutdown was somehow final, and many people expected Dawson to die out with its stubborn old-time residents.

Driving Points for YCGC

Story and photos by John Calam

[**Editor's note:** *John Calam is an emeritus professor in the Department of Education at the University of British Columbia.*]

When World War II was over in 1945, I left the Royal Canadian Air Force and enrolled at the University of British Columbia. While attending UBC, I landed a summer job with the Yukon Consolidated Gold Corporation. I was hired in the spring of 1947, and spent a memorable four months as a point driver for YCGC on a creek near Dawson City.

After taking my exams that spring, I bought a good pair of hobnailed boots, stuffed work clothes and a light sleeping robe into the bag of a Trapper Nelson packboard and hitched a ride to the Vancouver airport. A twin-engine Lockheed Lodestar flew me and other Vancouver YCGC summer recruits to Whitehorse, then on to Dawson. I recall the Dawson landing strip was very wet. As the wheels touched down, plumes of water shot into the air and we were greatly relieved when the plane came to a stop.

A company vehicle took us by way of Dominion Creek to Granville, where we were assigned to a bunkhouse. We met company foremen who explained the eight-hours-a-day, seven-days-a-week routine necessary because of the short working season. We learned something of the stripping, thawing, dredging and maintenance aspects of a commercial placer mining operation. We ate a cookhouse meal. Then we tentatively greeted one another since there were few prior acquaintances in the group.

At Granville the gold was chiefly located at bedrock level, up to 60 feet down. Stripping crews would clear trees and scrub the creek bed, using great jets of water from hydraulic monitors to erode the unfrozen overburden down to permafrost. Water for these impressive nozzles as well as for the thawing points was delivered through pipes fed from ditches high enough up the surrounding

The author (seated, second from right) poses with other members of the Yukon Consolidated crew in 1947.

hills to ensure sufficient pressure. Once stripped, the area would be thawed. In earlier days, workers used steam for thawing. But too-rapid thawing could dangerously undermine the ground and scald men, engulf machinery or cause other more serious accidents. By 1947, the custom was to thaw by means of cold water injected at pressure through narrow iron pipes. These were called points and those whose job it was to work them into the permafrost were point drivers. Except for the top foot or so, which would freeze up each winter, thawed ground remained soft for several years.

The final process was dredging the thawed ground. An enormous digging machine with a continuous chain of heavy steel buckets supported up front floated in its own dredge pond. It ate its way forward, ingesting thawed pay dirt, sluicing out placer gold and eliminating useless tailings. Gnawing away in front and ejecting tailings behind, it thus carried its dredge pond along with it.

The "point" was an iron pipe threaded at one end to receive a gooseneck connection and rubber hose, and armed at the other end with a chisel point and two apertures squirting water at 30 pounds' pressure. These points were coupled with feeder pipes charged, through main arteries, with ditch water. Spaced two or three yards apart according to a previous survey, the points were eased into the frozen ground to stand

Testing the depth of the thawed ground could be a headache for the man underneath if the man holding the sledgehammer slipped. Here, the author (right) holds a steel bar with a clamp while a co-worker wields the sledge.

vertically, infusing the surrounding permafrost with cold water. As the ground gradually thawed, the point driver twisted each point farther into the creek bed, using a clamp fitted with wooden handles and easily bolted on or detached.

Sometimes the point struck a rock. Then the point driver tightened his clamp and fitted the hammer. This was a grooved steel cylinder resting on the clamp, enveloping the pipe and secured by means of a horizontal pin. The driver had to grasp the pin with both hands, slide the hammer up the pipe and bring it down against the clamp with great force. If he was lucky, the rock split, allowing the point to work deeper. If unlucky, the rock resisted. The point had to be uprooted with a point jack, a heavy lever with chain attachment. An undamaged point could be restarted a foot or so from its initial spot, but if damaged, it had to be turned over to the blacksmith for repairs and a new point substituted.

In established thawing areas, point drivers walked up and down the rows easing, banging or otherwise persuading points farther into the ground. When each point was driven down to its gooseneck, they would turn off the water, attach a second length of pipe and restore the flow. Where I worked, we penetrated about four pipes or 40 feet, although the terrain varied in length either way in the region as a whole. When fully in place, points, extensions, goosenecks and hoses were left to do their thawing and new areas set up the same way.

Eventually, we tested for thawing, employing a solid steel bar and sledgehammer. From his ladder, the bar man drove the bar into the ground. Using a sledgehammer, the tip of the bar had to be driven to a predetermined depth to indicate satisfactory thawing. When this depth was reached, meaning that thawing had been properly achieved, the water was turned off and the points were yanked out and replanted elsewhere. I should add that as the bar man swung his sledge, someone had to steady the bar by holding the clamp. In those day, nobody wore protective headgear. It was heaven help the holder if the bar man aborted his blow and dropped the sledgehammer.

During thawing, a given section was rapidly transformed from secure footing to uncertain swamp. My boots, which I had treated inside and out with a concoction of neat's-foot oil and wax, kept out water remarkably well for hobnailed footwear. Throughout the day, though, we wallowed in mud. Hammer handles, clamp handles, shovel handles, pipes, hoses, wrenches and jacks were slippery with ooze. Work gloves turned slimy, providing an unsure grip. Walking the main and feeder pipes proved particularly tricky, and we fell off time and again. Worse yet, mosquitoes and blackflies thrived in or near the puddles.

On a typical work day, we woke early in the 20-place bunkhouse. On account of long daylight hours, southerners slept fitfully in any case. Given the primitive facilities, washing occupied little time or attention.

I remember breakfast — in fact, all meals — with pleasure. Danny, the company cook, furnished good fare. I developed a passion for canned peaches, hotcakes with bacon, drenched in melted butter and maple syrup, augmented with toast and raspberry jam, the lot helped down with generous mugs of coffee. We ate as though any doubts about wage rates could be allayed through serious eating — a sort of daily payment in kind. These stupendous breakfasts complemented ample bag lunches consumed out on the job and huge suppers whose quality, variety and sheer supply beggared description.

Shortly after breakfast — about 7:30 a.m. — we boarded an ancient open Ford truck with a capacity of about 16. With us rode John Blindheim, our foreman. A compact, strong man who could outlift any two of us, John relied on practical leadership and common sense to see that we earned our pay.

Throughout the summer, one work day felt much like the next. Once in the creek bed, we tended our points, driving them deeper, attaching extension pipes, adjusting valves, bashing reluctant points with the grooved hammer, pulling up stuck, bent or broken points and replacing them. Once in awhile we found that a point wouldn't go down any farther because sand or silt had plugged up the jets.

When this happened, we shouted across the flats for the point doctor, whose job it

This photo shows the thawing field from atop the main pipe. One of the smaller feeder pipes heads off to the right, while a forest of points is visible in the background. The ground is covered with mud.

was to shut off the water, remove the gooseneck and insert through the extensions and point a thin, flexible tube delivering a high-pressure jet of water, which in most cases cleared the obstruction.

On these work crews with their

different tasks, the greener pastures outlook prevailed. Point drivers thought point doctors had an easy time of it. They in turn believed ditch walkers had it made. Ditch walkers simply patrolled the ditch, removing the odd twig or dead bird that might clog up the system somewhere along the line. Ditch walkers doubtless envied truck drivers or dredgemasters or foreman and so on. Indeed, the collective height above ground level of any man's points revealed his progress at a glance. Shirking unobserved wasn't easy.

Many mornings were quite cold and bare hands on metal were uncomfortable. But as June matured, it warmed up and by late June we stripped to the waist and tanned. This was vanity at a price. Mosquitoes of legendary size and ferocity rendered any two-handed task tentative because one hand was constantly needed for slapping. Suicidal blackflies simply alighted and bit. When you were momentarily obliged to use two hands, blackflies would accumulate like a dark swatch on your arm. When at length you wiped them off, you left streaks of fresh blood.

Most of us let hair and beards grow to get a little face protection. Smudge fires of wet leaves and even old rubber tires helped a bit, though at times the smoke was worse than the flies.

The first few days of manual labor laid many university students on their ears. By the second week, however, we were getting the hang of things. As I look back, I am struck by the great amount of help we received from the regular crew. As the season progressed, we learned from them how to pace ourselves through eight hours of strenuous effort, plastered in mud, bathed in sweat, pestered by flies, burned by the high sun. We learned how to lift with straight backs and bent knees; how to let the hammer or the heavy jack handle do the work for us; how to connect two threaded pipes on the first try without cross-threading; how to attach the clamp at a convenient height, to get a good wide grip on the handles; and to lean over and twist evenly rather than petulantly assaulting the point. Most important, we learned from experienced men how to take in stride our own changing moods, so that a mere bent pipe or clogged hose did not become some sort of personal defeat.

Pacing aside, we were tired at the end of a shift and glad to sit down on a pile of pipe or timber, awaiting the old truck which would ferry us back to Granville. At the bunkhouse, we could rest up, wash or shower and check the mail. (The arrival of the mail was always a great event. Picking it up, reading it and replying assumed great importance.) Restored somewhat, we'd troop into the cookhouse to enjoy a meal which might include soup, juice, steak, stew, chicken, fish, vegetables, fruit, or pie, depending on the day and our appetites.

The author lived and worked in the Granville Camp during summer 1947. The cookhouse is the large building on the right; the work truck is parked in front of the bunkhouses on the left.

On most evenings we retired early, following a bit of laundry, maybe a game of cards or horseshoes or some reading or letter writing. Around 10:30 p.m., in broad daylight, we would start turning in, and by 11:00 p.m., with darkness yet to come, the bunkhouse would fall silent except for snores.

Leisure hours called for imagination. There was really very little spare time. Each day was a work day. If you took a day off, you lost a day's pay. Some considered the odd trip to Dawson well worth the loss. Returning, they would speak fondly of stores, saloons, movies and high-stakes card games. Several praised affable Dawson prostitutes whose repertoires included repairing torn shirts, resewing buttons and darning socks. But most men decided to hoard slim resources, finding their entertainment closer to camp during the long evening light.

Every week or so, a truck loaded with cigarettes, soap, work clothes, toothpaste, magazines and patent medicines lurched into camp. We could buy these and other items and have the purchase price deducted from our wages as "sundries." But mostly we assembled merely to see the sundries truck arrive and depart.

Some evenings we played records on a gramophone we all helped purchase. Or we just wandered around camp. Mosquitoes aside, summer nights were magnificent. The growing season was

Two visiting artists sketch their surroundings as a local youngster looks on.

short but dramatic. One June evening the hillsides were gray. The next they were aspen green. Wildflowers appeared in sudden bursts. A company straw-boss residing nearby planted tomatoes, nurturing them in a makeshift frame-and-plastic greenhouse. We inspected them every night or so as in unfailing light they soared to seven or eight feet tall.

We sometimes dropped by the cookhouse, where Danny set out a late evening snack featuring delicious fruit pies. And we yarned, and we sang, "Sweet Adeline," "Down By the Old Mill Stream," "Sing Us Another One," "North Atlantic Squadron," "Last Night I Slept in a Hollow Log" and other tunes.

One social highlight was the arrival of two young ladies who visited the camp, staying with the family who grew the tomatoes. They were landscape artists retained, I think, by a railroad company (possibly the White Pass and Yukon) to paint scenes to brighten up the passenger cars. When they worked outside on camp stools, dabbing brushes on palettes, or showed up for incidental meals as cookhouse guests, one might have

The author and his fellow workers were hauled to and from the dredging fields in the Granville Camp work truck.

expected untoward teasing. On the contrary, the effect on the crew was beneficial. We watched our language, laundered our work shirts, trimmed our beards and looked to our table manners. Today, we would be open to charges of reverse chauvinism. Yesterday it seemed the thing to do.

Softball also helped to pass the time. Several dredge-loop communities exchanged bush-league games and we entered as the Granville Beavers. As a confessed cricketer, I was put safely out in right field where usually nothing much happened owing to the cunning of our pitcher, the rutted state of the average infield and the predilection of more astute batters for bunts and shorter base hits. Once I caught a specatcular high fly

which, in cricket, would have stopped play for a moment. "Home it!" screamed my colleagues. Unfamiliar with the request, I walked over to the mound to deliver the caught ball, feeling very proud. Two Dominion Creekers on base raced in for runs. We lost. I was never asked back.

One evening in late August, several of us engaged in an argument about pioneers. We resolved not to leave Granville before having accomplished some original feat. Since every conceivable placer-mining gambit had, we thought, already been made, we decided to fly the first homemade box kite on Dominion Creek. We split long sticks for uprights, shorter ones for crosspieces. From Danny's cookhouse we liberated string for lashing, brown paper for sail and flour and canned milk for paste. The result was a six-foot beauty — a veritable hand-burner given sufficient pull.

Whether our kite was really the first on Dominion Creek remains unverified. But it certainly flew. Fresh late-summer winds bore it up the full 400-foot length of the stopgap line knotted together from uneven pieces of twine. As an added novelty, we flew this YCGC special with a penlight attached to the frame so it would shine down. We flew our kite many times toward the end of the summer. The last I saw of it was, in fact, the day I left. We had pegged it out on full string and could see it riding high above the creek bed awaiting calm or rain, which would inevitably bring it down one final time.

I recall many of us wished away those last dozen days in the mud and nights in the bunkhouse. We even converted them to hours and minutes or expressed them as pencil tallies on the bunkhouse wall. An inventive, ever-hungry pal translated them into breakfast hotcakes at six per morning. But finally the time arrived when my packboard was hoisted into the truck and I with it.

Why I didn't take the sternwheeler from Dawson to Whitehorse I shall never know, and now that the option is no longer available, I regret the decision. Instead I flew to Whitehorse. From there I rode the narrow gauge White Pass and Yukon Route Railway to Skagway.

The next morning I boarded a ship headed south down the Inside Passage. My career as a point driver in the Yukon was over.

Modern Times

D awson's still there. I first saw it in August 1981, from a raft at the end of a trip down the Pelly and Yukon rivers. Oddly enough, river traffic was making a comeback. Recreational boaters were vacationing along the shores of the Yukon and its tributaries. Dawson made a natural destination. I was, in a way, one of the people who saved Dawson.

They weren't all boaters. The first of them were federal government officials, who decided to turn Dawson's history into a gold mine of another sort and try to attract more tourists. In league with Dawson's business-

Tourists and residents turn out for the festivities on Discovery Day, a Yukon holiday commemorating the discovery of gold in the Klondike on August 17, 1896. The celebration includes the Yukon Order of Pioneers' parade, ball games and dances.
(Steve McCutcheon)

A modern-day miner uses a hydraulic monitor to wash out gold-bearing gravel. (Steve McCutcheon)

Tailing piles left behind by relentless dredges fill the valley of the Klondike River just outside Dawson. (Rollo Pool, staff)

A young tourist tries out a gold pan at Guggieville, an attraction located at the junction of the Klondike Loop Highway and Bonanza Road, on the former site of Yukon Gold Company's camp. (Janet Klein)

No visit to Dawson is complete without a stop at Robert Service's cabin to hear a local actor recite such poems as The Cremation of Sam McGee *and* The Shooting of Dan McGrew. *Service lived in the cabin from 1909 until 1912, when he left Dawson. Parks Canada has restored the landmark from its once run-down condition, shown in the photo taken in June 1950 (inset).* (Janet Klein; inset, Steve McCutcheon)

Klondike Visitors Association operates Diamond Tooth Gertie's Gambling Hall, one of Dawson's most popular attractions, in the old Arctic Brotherhood Hall. (Chlaus Lotscher)

men, who had formed the Klondike Visitors Association, they staged in 1962 the Dawson City Festival for the Arts. The Palace Grand Theater was reconstructed at a cost of $300,000 and an off-Broadway play staged. A shallow-draft steamboat named the SS *Keno* was used as a dance hall. The festival was not a financial success, but it did bring more than 18,000 people to Dawson.

The next year, though, tourism dropped off to 4,500 and, although it increased from there, was not the gold mine first envisioned. A gloomy 1964 government report on Dawson found, "The city now has one customer for sewer and water for every four lots." To bolster the tourist trade, gambling was legalized on a limited basis in 1971. The old Arctic Brotherhood Hall, which had served Laura Berton and her contemporaries as Versailles, was turned into a casino named after one of the rush's hurdy-gurdy girls, Diamond Tooth Gertie.

In 1967, the United States let the price of gold float. As the price rose, activity in the goldfields increased. In 1980, when gold hit a high of more than $800 an ounce, the fields boomed. Although gold was about half that price in the summer of 1987, there were claims being worked and few for sale.

The Arctic Brotherhood Hall was not the only building to be rehabilitated. The federal government, through Parks Canada, committed millions of dollars to the restoration of gold rush-era buildings. These restorations were difficult and expensive because the structures had been put on permafrost. The permanently frozen ground moved and buckled, leaving the buildings at crazy angles. Workmen had to level them and put in foundations to stabilize them. The restored buildings will be part of the Klondike Gold Rush Historical Park. "Parks Canada's massive investment in the Dawson Historic Site project revitalized the gold rush town as a tourist attraction," historian Kenneth Coates wrote. ". . . the programme doubtlessly saved the community from ignominious disintegration."

That work continues; eventually, some two dozen buildings will be restored. In the summer of 1987, YCGC's Bear Creek camp was reopened as a tourist stop. There are hotels and campgrounds, motor home parks and bakeries, a museum, saloons and cafes. Dawson has turned itself into a tourist attraction. It seems to working. In July 1987, more than 30,000 people toured the SS *Keno*.

The gold rush comes to Dawson every summer now.

The Dawson Post Office, built at the turn of the century, has been completely restored by Parks Canada. (Jerrianne Lowther, staff)

St. Mary's Church, the first Roman Catholic church in Dawson, was originally located along the waterfront in 1897, then moved to the building shown here in the 1920s. (Mike Doogan)

The SS Keno, last steamer to run the Yukon River, operated along the river between 1922 and 1960. Today she has been restored and is open daily during the summer for guided tours. (Rollo Pool, staff)

Dawson City Sourdoughs

By Ron Wendt

[**Editor's note:** *The Klondike gold rush drew men of many nationalities and backgrounds to the Yukon. As John McPhee wrote in* Coming Into The Country *(1977), ". . . .half the Tower of Babel was . . . in the goldfields." Most of these early gold seekers left the North, but a few stayed on, and fewer still were born in the North of pioneer parents. Part-time miner Ron Wendt has talked with some of these old-timers and here shares a few insights into Dawson City's more enduring citizens.*]

Mike Wineage

In his last years roaming the streets of Dawson City, Mike Wineage, known to locals as Black Mike, collected sticks for his fireplace and bones for his dog. Mike was 107 when he died in a Dawson nursing home in 1977.

Six feet, two inches, with a full black beard, Mike was from Yugoslavia and came to the United States in the late 1890s. He settled around Butte, Montana, where he became involved in the labor movement. Many Slavs were working in the mines around Butte when the sheriff shot and killed the local leader of their labor group. The sheriff left town for a while, but when he returned a group of Slavs, including Mike, were waiting for him. The sheriff was killed, and Mike left Montana.

In 1906 Mike hit the streets of Dawson City. He made his living as a woodcutter, and occasionally he headed out to the creeks to work in the mines.

Mike eventually married a woman of the line whom the townspeople called "Rain in the Face" because her face was so wrinkled. The couple lived in a wood camp up the Klondike River.

When Mike died, there was a big turnout for his funeral. His casket was carried to the hole where a pallbearer had to step onto a board across the open grave. The board suddenly broke, sending the man, casket and board sideways into the hole.

"I rushed over to the casket and gee . . . here's Mike out of the box!" recalled Dawson old-timer Windy Farr. "The casket had popped open. The minister didn't know what to do so a few of us put Mike back."

Black Mike's beard was all trimmed, he was dressed in a suit, and he looked fine according to most of his friends, who thought he looked better in death than in life. When the funeral was over, the people didn't know whether to laugh or cry.

One of his close friends said, "Mike would have wanted it this way!"

Dawson City sourdough "Black Mike" Wineage enjoys the festivities at Discovery Days in 1976. (David Rhode)

Will DeWolfe

Will DeWolfe was born March 28, 1908, in Dawson City, and has spent most of his life in this area. A dog-team driver and horse freighter, Will is the son of the Yukon's famous mail carrier, Percy DeWolfe. From 1915 to 1950, Percy hauled mail along the Yukon River between Dawson City and Eagle, earning the nickname, "Iron Man of the North." Will worked with his father, hauling mail and sometimes passengers.

The DeWolfes had a fish camp about 25 miles downstream from Dawson and spent most of their summers there. Today, all that remains of the DeWolfe camp are dilapidated log cabins, built around 1905.

Will DeWolfe remembers: "We kept the horses in our big stables back at the fish camp, or Halfway House, they used to call it. We had two horses. I drove one, and Dad drove the other. Dad used to drive the horses double, but toward the end he used to drive them single, hooked up to a sleigh.

"He drowned five sets of horses between Dawson and Eagle. About 23 miles from Eagle, they broke through the ice. He had 22 sacks of mail that went

Old-timer Will DeWolfe, dog-team driver and horse freighter, hauled freight and passengers from Dawson City to Walker Fork in the Fortymile district in the 1930s. He is now retired and living in Dawson. (Ron Wendt)

down. . . . Dad had to walk seven miles to a roadhouse."

On one other trip, Will's father broke through the ice near Halfway House and drowned two horses.

"Back in his day and mine, it was nothing but horse and dog team delivering the mail. We had a nice, wide, packed trail down the Yukon for our horses. Each horse had its own sleigh. When we came to open water, we'd test the ice in front of the horse with an ax. Dad used to use snowshoes on horses. You could go 25 miles a day with a horse. In summer we'd haul freight with 30-foot boats equipped with 25-horsepower marine motors."

Will used to haul passengers on sleds pulled by dog teams between Dawson City and Walkers Fork, in the Fortymile, during the 1930s. His route took him via Steele and Canyon creeks.

"I ran nine dogs when I was hauling, all big huskies. The lightest dog I had was 80 pounds. Most of them were 100 pounds. We could take two passengers up to the Fork. It used to take me two days to run to the Fork. Coming back I'd make faster time because of the empty sled. It was a tough climb to get into Walkers Fork and out of Canyon Creek.

Will recalls the town of Fortymile in the 1930s, and the few residents who lived there. There were about six people there then, including a policeman, customs agent, storekeeper and hotel operator.

A portion of the town is located on an island separated by a slough which runs from the Yukon to the Fortymile River near its mouth. The hotel, run by Al Schultz, was across the slough from the town. Will says it was better than any hotel in Dawson, but it burned down.

"Schultz, Dave Swanson, Ben Finks, Art Anderson and Pete Anderson, they're all dead," says Will. "They all lived there. The big mission house on the island could be seen from a long way off, but it was washed downstream [by] high water. That was in the '40s, I guess. There used to be a lot of buildings on that island."

Will had many jobs throughout his life, including working the dredges on Bonanza and Dominion creeks.

"I used to watch that stacker belt where the tailings went out. . . . [The stacker belt conveyed excess gravels out of the dredges where they were dumped in tailing piles. In some cases, gold nuggets more than an inch square passed through the belts and were dumped out in the tailings.] We had four men to a shift: winchman, oiler, two deckmen, one in the bow and one in the stern. We only got 45 cents an hour in those days."

The old-timer worked on road crews for a few years, building portions of the Taylor Highway which runs from the Alaska Highway at Tetlin Junction to Eagle on the Yukon River. When he was not working the roads in winter, Will would trap up the Fifteenmile River below Dawson.

"The Fifteenmile River country was rocky with high hills. There were a lot of foxes, marten and beaver up there. I used to trap about 25 miles up and did some prospecting. I was the one who discovered asbestos up there and on Cassiar and Clinton creeks. I was called the Asbestos King."

Across from Halfway House, Will found another outcrop of asbestos. He never fooled around with gold as a means of making a living, but he keeps samples of all his asbestos finds around his cabin and can identify the source of every piece.

"That's why they [locals of Dawson and surrounding areas] call me the Asbestos King. But I only got $10,000 out of all of it. A big company took over my mines at Cassiar Creek. I sold to Con West [Consolidated West] for $10,000."

Most recently, Will worked for Parks Canada at Fortymile, using Swanson's General Store as his office.

"I had a big guest book there for visitors to sign. They'd come from Germany, and all over Alaska and Canada. Over 200 people pass through in a year. Some came down the Yukon, while others rafted the Fortymile.

"As long as I've been around Dawson, it's changed a lot. There's lots of new houses going up, and the old buildings coming down. Everybody's changing. All those guys I knew died off, I guess. There aren't too many left. I was born and raised in Dawson and will probably die here."

Epilogue

Once crammed with stampeders' tents, the Dawson waterfront now provides moorage for small boats and floatplanes. (Leslie Barber)

Much of the gold is gone, dug out by picks or giant machines, sorted, smelted into bars, gone wherever gold goes. Some is being dug out as you read this, washed down by monitors or chewed out by bulldozers. The mother lode, if it exists, has yet to be found.

Many of the Indians are gone. From their first contact population of about 1,000, the Han have decreased to about 250, killed by disease and alcohol and despair. The biggest group lives near Eagle. They never had a big part in the rush or what followed; it wasn't until the 1950s that any lived in Dawson.

The prospectors are gone. Al Mayo in 1923, Robert Henderson, who got a share of the fame but none of the money from the Klondike discovery, died of cancer in 1933. George

Although Parks Canada and other organizations have done much to restore the flavor of the gold rush to Dawson, some skeletons of the old days remain. One such structure is Strait's Auction House, built in 1901 and today one of the most photographed buildings in town.
(Mike Doogan)

Present-day visitors to Dawson City arrive by way of the Klondike Loop Highway, crossing the Yukon River on the government-operated ferry the **George Black**. *(Jim Green)*

Carmack, who got the fame and the money, died in Vancouver in 1922.

The gold kings are gone. Tom Lippy lost heavily in several schemes, including one to develop the Katalla oil fields near Cordova. He died in Seattle in 1931. Clarence Berry had better luck with oil, investing his Klondike fortune in California fields that made him even more money. He died of appendicitis in San Francisco in 1930. Most of the others died broke.

The stampeders are gone; after all, 90 years have passed since they set out. Alfred McMichael, who left the North in 1899, committed suicide in Detroit in 1907. Martha Black, who stayed and went on to serve in the Canadian Parliament herself, died in Whitehorse in 1957.

The cabins and sluices and caches are gone, many of them eaten by the ponderous, relentless dredges. The dredges themselves are gone, except for some skeletons and one restored as a tourist attraction. So is the Twelvemile Ditch, except for a scar more than 70 miles long. Even the creeks are gone in parts, diverted by mining operations.

What remains are mainly the memories.

Memories have become Dawson's stock-in-trade, pleasant memories, full of bizarre people and loony doings. Life in Dawson may have been hard and dark and dirty, but what survives are stories of bright lights and laughter. The place is helped, not haunted, by its past.

There are no ghosts in Dawson City.

Bibliography

Adney, Tappan. *The Klondike Stampede of 1897-1898.* New York: Harper and Brothers, 1900.

Aigner, Jean; Guthrie, Mary Lee; Guthrie, R. Dale; Nelson, Richard K.; Schneider, William S.; and Thorson, Robert M. *Interior Alaska: A Journey Through Time.* Anchorage: The Alaska Geographic Society, 1986.

Alaska Geographic Society, The. *Alaska's Oil/Gas and Minerals Industry.* Alaska Geographic, Vol. 9, No. 4, 1982.

Alaska Geographic Society, The. *Northwest Territories.* Alaska Geographic, Vol. 12, No. 1, 1985.

Alberts, Laurie. "Petticoats and Pickaxes." *The Alaska Journal*® Vol. 7, No. 3: pages 146-159.

Berton, Laura Beatrice. *I Married the Klondike.* Boston: Little, Brown and Company, 1954.

Berton, Pierre. *My Country.* Toronto: McClelland and Stewart, 1976.

—. *The Klondike Fever.* New York: Alfred A. Knopf, 1958.

—. *The Klondike Quest.* Boston/Toronto: Little, Brown and Co., 1983.

Black, Martha Louise. *Martha Black.* Anchorage: Alaska Northwest Publishing Co., 1986.

Bolotin, Norm. *Klondike Lost.* Anchorage: Alaska Northwest Publishing Co., 1980.

Burlingame, Virginia S. "John J. Healy's Alaskan Adventure." *The Alaska Journal*® Vol. 8, No. 4: pages 310-319.

Bush, Edward F. "Robert W. Service: Bard of the Klondike." *The Alaska Journal*® Vol. 4, No. 2: pages 105-112.

Buske, Frank E. "Sam Dunham, Forgotten Gold Rush Poet." In *The Alaska Journal*®, *A 1981 Collection,* pages 126-133. Anchorage: Alaska Northwest Publishing Co., 1981.

Cadell, H.M. *The Klondike and Yukon Goldfield in 1913.* Seattle: The Shorey Book Store, 1964.

Canada Bureau of Northwest Territories and Yukon Affairs. *The Yukon Territory.* Ottawa, 1944.

Canada Department of the Interior. *Yukon Territory 1926.* Ottawa, 1926.

Clifford, Howard. *The Skagway Story.* Anchorage: Alaska Northwest Publishing Co., 1975.

Coates, Kenneth. *Canada's Colonies.* Toronto: James Lorimer and Co., 1985.

Cohen, Stan. *The White Pass and Yukon Route.* Missoula, Mont.: Pictorial Histories Publishing Co., 1980.

Cole, Terrence. "Klondike Visions." In *The Alaska Journal*®, *A 1986 Collection,* pages 82-93. Anchorage: Alaska Northwest Publishing Co., 1986.

Cooke, Alan, and Holland, Olive. *The Exploration of Northern Canada.* Toronto: The Arctic History Press, 1978.

Dall, W.H.; Dawson, George M.; and Ogilvie, William. *The Yukon Territory.* New York: AMS Press, 1975.

DeArmond, R.N. "Gold on the Fortymile." *The Alaska Journal*® Vol. 3, No. 2: pages 114-121.

Dial, Scott. "The Gold Rush Saloon." *The Alaska Journal*® Vol. 5, No. 2: pages 81-88.

Dunham, Sam. *The Alaska Gold Fields.* Anchorage: Alaska Northwest Publishing Co., 1983.

Green, Lewis. *The Gold Hustlers.* Anchorage: Alaska Northwest Publishing Co., 1977.

Hahn, Kavik W. "White Death on the Chilkoot." In *The Alaska Journal*®, *A 1981 Collection,* pages 50-65. Anchorage: Alaska Northwest Publishing Co., 1981.

Helm, June, ed. *Handbook of North American Indians.* Vol. 6, Subarctic. Washington, D.C.: Smithsonian Institution, 1981.

Holloway, Sam. *Klondike Kate.* Whitehorse: Lone Wolf Press, 1987.

Hunt, John Clark. "The Adventures of the Iowa Goldseekers." *The Alaska Journal*® Vol. 3, No. 1: pages 2-11.

Hunt, William R. *North of 53°.* New York: MacMillan Publishing Co., 1974.

Ingersoll, Ernest. *Gold Fields of the Klondike.* Langley, B.C.: Mr. Paperback, 1981.

James, J.R. *The Great Canadian Outback.* Vancouver, B.C.: Douglas and McIntyre, 1978.

Lotz, J.R. *The Dawson Area.* Ottawa: Department of Northern Affairs and National Resources, 1964.

McCourt, Edward. *The Yukon and Northwest Territories.* New York: St. Martin's Press, 1969.

McQuesten, Leroy N. *Recollections of Leroy N. McQuesten.* Dawson City, Y.T.: Yukon Order of Pioneers, 1977.

Morgan, Murray. *One Man's Gold Rush.* Seattle: University of Washington Press, 1967.

Nelson, Arnold and Helen. "Bringing Home the Gold." *The Alaska Journal*® Vol. 9, No. 3: pages 52-59.

—. "The Dazzle of Gold at #16 Eldorado." In *The Alaska Journal*®, *A 1981 Collection,* pages 8-17. Anchorage: Alaska Northwest Publishing Co., 1981.

—. "The Bubble of Oil at Katalla." In *The Alaska Journal*®, *A 1981 Collection,* pages 18-27. Anchorage: Alaska Northwest Publishing Co., 1981.

Nicholls, Richard E., and Teacher, Lawrence, eds. *The Unabridged Jack London.* Philadelphia: Running Press, 1981.

Ogilvie, William. *The Klondike Official Guide.* Toronto: The Hunter Rose Co., 1898.

Osgood, Cornelius. *The Han Indians. A Compilation of Ethnographic and Historical Data on the Alaska-Yukon Boundary Area.* Department of Anthropology, Yale University, 1971.

Oswald, E.T., and Senyk, J.P. *Ecoregions of the Yukon Territory.* Victoria, B.C.; Canadian Forestry Service, 1977.

Pitcher, James S. *Sourdough Jim Pitcher.* Anchorage: Alaska Northwest Publishing Co., 1985.

Reinicker, Juliette C., ed. *Klondike Letters.* Anchorage: Alaska Northwest Publishing Co., 1984.

Remley, David A. *Crooked Road: The Story of the Alaska Highway.* New York: McGraw-Hill Book Co., 1976.

Sack, Doug. *Gold: A Brief History of Dawson City and the Klondike.* Dawson City, Y.T.: The Monte Carlo Limited, 1979.

Satterfield, Archie. *After the Gold Rush.* Philadelphia: J.B. Lippincott Co., 1976.

—. *Chilkoot Pass.* Anchorage: Alaska Northwest Publishing Co., 1973.

Schwatka, Frederick. *Along Alaska's Great River.* Anchorage: Alaska Northwest Publishing Co., 1983.

Scidmore, Eliza Ruhamah. "The Northwest Passages to the Yukon." *The Alaska Journal*® Vol. 3, No. 3: pages 144-146.

Service, Robert. *The Trail of '98.* New York: Grossett and Dunlap, 1910.

Stevens, Gary. "Arizona Charlie's Floating Opera House." *The Alaska Journal*® Vol. 15, No. 3: pages 14-20.

Warner, Iris. "Pioneer Banking at Dawson." *The Alaska Journal*® Vol. 1, No. 2: pages 41-48.

Webb, Melody. *The Last Frontier.* Albuquerque: University of New Mexico Press, 1985.

—. "Steamboats on the Yukon River." *The Alaska Journal*® Vol. 15, No. 3: pages 21-29.

Index

Alaska Geographic® Back Issues

The North Slope, Vol. 1, No. 1. Charter issue. *Out of print.*

One Man's Wilderness, Vol. 1, No. 2. *Out of print.* (Book edition available, $19.95.)

Admiralty . . . Island in Contention, Vol. 1, No. 3. In-depth review of Southeast's Admiralty Island. 78 pages, $5.

Fisheries of the North Pacific: History, Species, Gear & Processes, Vol. 1, No. 4. *Out of print.* (Book edition available, $24.95.)

The Alaska-Yukon Wild Flowers Guide, Vol. 2, No. 1. *Out of print.* (Book edition available, $12.95.)

Richard Harrington's Yukon, Vol. 2, No. 2. *Out of print.*

Prince William Sound, Vol. 2, No. 3. *Out of print.*

Yakutat: The Turbulent Crescent, Vol. 2, No. 4. *Out of print.*

Glacier Bay: Old Ice, New Land, Vol. 3, No. 1. *Out of print.*

The Land: Eye of the Storm, Vol. 3, No. 2. *Out of print.*

Richard Harrington's Antarctic, Vol. 3, No. 3. Reviews Antarctica and islands of southern polar regions, territories of mystery and controversy. Fold-out map. 104 pages, $8.95.

The Silver Years of the Alaska Canned Salmon Industry: An Album of Historical Photos, Vol. 3, No. 4. *Out of print.*

Alaska's Volcanoes: Northern Link in the Ring of Fire, Vol. 4, No. 1. *Out of print.*

The Brooks Range: Environmental Watershed, Vol. 4, No. 2. *Out of print.*

Kodiak: Island of Change, Vol. 4, No. 3. *Out of print.*

Wilderness Proposals: Which Way for Alaska's Lands?, Vol. 4, No. 4. *Out of print.*

Cook Inlet Country, Vol. 5, No. 1. *Out of print.*

Southeast: Alaska's Panhandle, Vol. 5, No. 2. Explores southeastern Alaska's maze of fjords and islands, forests and mountains, from Dixon Entrance to Icy Bay, including all of the Inside Passage. The book profiles every town, and reviews the region's history, economy, people, attractions and future. Fold-out map. 192 pages, $12.95.

Bristol Bay Basin, Vol. 5, No. 3. *Out of print.*

Alaska Whales and Whaling, Vol. 5, No. 4. The wonders of whales in Alaska — their life cycles, travels and travails — are examined, with an authoritative history of commercial and subsistence whaling in the North. Includes a fold-out poster of 14 major whale species in Alaska in perspective, color photos and illustrations, with historical photos and line drawings. 144 pages, $19.95.

Yukon-Kuskokwim Delta, Vol. 6, No. 1. *Out of print.*

The Aurora Borealis, Vol. 6, No. 2. Explores the northern lights in history and today; their cause, how they work, and their importance in contemporary science. 96 pages, $7.95.

Alaska's Native People, Vol. 6, No. 3. Examines the worlds of the Inupiat and Yupik Eskimo, Athabascan, Aleut, Tlingit, Haida and Tsimshian. Fold-out map of Native villages and language areas. 304 pages, $24.95.

The Stikine River, Vol. 6, No. 4. River route to three Canadian gold strikes, the Stikine is the largest and most navigable of several rivers that flow from northwestern Canada through southeastern Alaska to the Pacific Ocean. Fold-out map. 96 pages, $9.95.

Alaska's Great Interior, Vol. 7, No. 1. Examines the people, communites, economy, and wilderness of Alaska's rich Interior, the immense valley between the Alaska Range and Brooks Range. Fold-out map. 128 pages, $9.95.

A Photographic Geography of Alaska, Vol. 7, No. 2. A visual tour through the six regions of Alaska: Southeast, Southcentral/Gulf Coast, Alaska Peninsula and Aleutians, Bering Sea Coast, Arctic and Interior. 192 pages, $15.95.

The Aleutians, Vol. 7, No. 3. Home of the Aleut, a tremendous wildlife spectacle, a major World War II battleground, and an important arm of Alaska's commercial fishing industry. Fold-out map. 224 pages, $14.95.

Klondike Lost: A Decade of Photographs by Kinsey & Kinsey, Vol. 7, No. 4. *Out of print.* (Book edition available, $12.95.)

Wrangell-Saint Elias, Vol. 8, No. 1. Alaska's only designated World Heritage Area, this mountain wilderness takes in the nation's largest national park in its sweep from the Copper River across the Wrangell Mountains to the southern tip of the Saint Elias Range near Yakutat. Fold-out map. 144 pages, $19.95.

Alaska Mammals, Vol. 8, No. 2. Reviews in anecdotes and facts the entire spectrum of Alaska's wildlife. 184 pages, $12.95.

The Kotzebue Basin, Vol. 8, No. 3. Examines northwestern Alaska's thriving trading area of Kotzebue Sound and the Kobuk and Noatak river basins. 184 pages, $12.95.

Alaska National Interest Lands, Vol. 8, No. 4. Reviews each of Alaska's national interest land (d-2 lands) selections, outlining location, size, access and briefly describes special attractions. 242 pages, $14.95.

Alaska's Glaciers, Vol. 9, No. 1. Examines in-depth the massive rivers of ice, their composition, exploration, present-day distribution and scientific significance. Illustrated with many contemporary color and historical black-and-white photos, the text includes separate discussions of more than a dozen glacial regions. 144 pages, $19.95

Sitka and Its Ocean/Island World, Vol. 9, No. 2. From the elegant capital of Russian America to a beautiful but modern port, Sitka, on Baranof Island, has become a commercial and cultural center for Southeastern Alaska. 128 pages, $19.95.

Islands of the Seals: The Pribilofs, Vol. 9, No. 3. Great herds of northern fur seals and immense flocks of seabirds share their island homeland with Aleuts brought to this remote Bering Sea outpost by Russians. 128 pages, $9.95.

Alaska's Oil/Gas & Minerals Industry, Vol. 9, No. 4. Experts detail the geological processes and resulting mineral and fossil fuel resources that contribute substantially to Alaska's economy. 216 pages, $12.95.

Adventure Roads North: The Story of the Alaska Highway and Other Roads in *The MILEPOST®*, Vol. 10, No. 1. Reviews the history of Alaska's roads and takes a mile-by-mile look at the country they cross. 224 pages, $14.95.

ANCHORAGE and the Cook Inlet Basin, Vol. 10, No. 2. Reviews in depth the commercial and urban center of the Last Frontier. Three fold-out maps. 168 pages, $14.95.

Alaska's Salmon Fisheries, Vol. 10, No. 3. A comprehensive look at Alaska's most valuable commercial fishery. 128 pages, $12.95.

Up the Koyukuk, Vol. 10, No. 4. Highlights the wildlife and traditional native lifestyle of this remote region of northcentral Alaska. 152 pages, $14.95.

Nome: City of the Golden Beaches, Vol. 11, No. 1. Reviews the colorful history of one of Alaska's most famous gold rush towns. 184 pages, $14.95.

Alaska's Farms and Gardens, Vol. 11, No. 2. An overview of the past, present and future of agriculture in Alaska, with details on growing your own vegetables in the North. 144 pages, $12.95.

Chilkat River Valley, Vol. 11, No. 3. Explores the mountain-rimmed valley at the head of the Inside Passage, its natural resources, and the residents who have settled there. 112 pages, $12.95.

Alaska Steam, Vol. 11, No. 4. Pictorial history of the pioneering Alaska Steamship Company. 160 pages, $12.95.

Northwest Territories, Vol. 12, No. 1. In-depth look at the magnificent wilderness of Canada's high Arctic. Fold-out map. 136 pages, $12.95.

Alaska's Forest Resources, Vol. 12, No. 2. Examines the botanical, recreational and economic value of Alaska's forests. 200 pages, $14.95.

Alaska Native Arts and Crafts, Vol. 12, No. 3. In-depth review of the art and artifacts of Alaska's Natives. 215 pages, $17.95.

Our Arctic Year, Vol. 12, No. 4. Compelling story of a year in the wilds of the Brooks Range. 150 pages, $12.95.

Where Mountains Meet the Sea: Alaska's Gulf Coast, Vol. 13, No. 1. Alaskan's first-hand descriptions of the 850-mile arc that crowns the Pacific Ocean from Kodiak to Cape Spencer at the entrance to southeastern Alaska's Inside Passage. 191 pages, $14.95.

Backcountry Alaska, Vol. 13, No. 2. A full-color look at the remote communities of Alaska. Companion volume to *The ALASKA WILDERNESS MILEPOST®.* 224 pages, $14.95.

British Columbia's Coast/The Canadian Inside Passage, Vol. 13, No. 3. Reviews the B.C. coast west of the Coast Mountain divide from mighty Vancouver and elegant Victoria in the south to the forested wilderness to the north, including the Queen Charlotte Islands. Fold-out map. 200 pages, $14.95.

Lake Clark/Lake Iliamna Country, Vol. 13, No. 4. Chronicles the human and natural history of the region that many claim has a sampling of all the best that Alaska has to offer in natural beauty. 152 pages, $14.95.

Dogs of the North, Vol. 14, No. 1. The first men to cross the Bering Land Bridge probably brought dogs to Alaska. This issue examines the development of northern breeds from the powerful husky and malemute to the fearless little Tahltan bear dog, the evolution of the dogsled, uses of dogs, and the history of sled-dog racing from the All-Alaska Sweepstakes of 1908 to the nationally televised Iditarod of today. 120 pages, $16.95.

South/Southeast Alaska, Vol. 14, No. 2. Reviews the natural and human resources of the southernmost tip of Alaska's Panhandle, from Sumner Strait to the Canadian border. Fold-out map. 120 pages, $14.95.

Alaska's Seward Peninsula, Vol. 14, No. 3. The Seward Peninsula is today's remnant of the Bering Land Bridge, gateway to an ancient America. This issue chronicles the blending of traditional Eskimo culture with the white man's persistent search for gold. Fold-out map. 112 pages, $14.95.

The Upper Yukon Basin, Vol. 14, No. 4. Yukoner Monty Alford describes this remote region, headwaters for one of the continent's mightiest rivers and gateway for some of Alaska's earliest pioneers. 117 pages, $14.95.

Glacier Bay: Icy Wilderness, Vol. 15, No. 1. Covers the 5,000-square-mile wilderness now known as Glacier Bay National Park and Preserve, including the natural and human history of the Glacier Bay area, its wildlife, how to get there, what to expect, and what changes now seem predictable. 103 pages, $14.95.

NEXT ISSUE:
Denali, Denali's Wife, Denali's Children, Vol. 15, No. 3. It was *Denali* to the Tanana Indians, *Doleika* to the nearby Tainanas, *Bolshaya Gora* to the Russians, all connoting size and height and scenic grandeur. A gold-prospector called it *McKinley* less than a century ago, and unfortunately that name endured. But the mountain massif in southcentral Alaska, by whatever name, has fascinated man from the primitive to the present. This book is an indepth guide to the Great One, its lofty neighbors and the surrounding wilderness now known as Denali National Park and Preserve.

ALL PRICES SUBJECT TO CHANGE.

Your $30 membership in The Alaska Geographic Society includes four subsequent issues of *ALASKA GEOGRAPHIC®*, the Society's official quarterly. Please add $4 for non-U.S. membership. Additional membership information is available upon request. Single copies of the *ALASKA GEOGRAPHIC®* back issues are also available. When ordering, please make payments in U.S. funds and add $1.50 postage/handling per copy. To order back issues send your check or money order and volumes desired to:

The Alaska Geographic Society

P.O. Box 93370, Anchorage, Alaska 99509